# A.A. Castor

# Israel

The Last Vestige of European Colonialism in the Middle East

# Table of Contents


Israel: The Last Vestige of European Colonialism in the Middle East........................................................................................1

Dedication ..........................................................................3

Copyright © 2024 by A.A. Castor .....................................4

Why I Am Writing This Book ............................................5

Warning and Disclaimer ...................................................7

About the Author...............................................................9

Introduction: Unveiling Colonial Roots.........................10

Chapter 1: Historical Background of Zionism and European......21

Chapter 2: Migration Patterns and Genetic Evidence....................37

Chapter 3: The Narrative of the 'Return' vs. Colonialism.............52

Chapter 4: Israel's Founding Myths and Reality............................67

Chapter 5: Marginalization of Indigenous Populations.................83

Chapter 6: Integration Challenges of Non-European Jewish Communities ............................................................................. 100

Chapter 7: Western Powers' Support of Israel............................. 118

Chapter 8: Reparations and Accountability ................................. 141

Chapter 9: The Modern Impact of European Colonial Legacy. 158

Chapter 10: Israel in the Context of Global Colonialism .......... 176

Conclusion....................................................................... 204

Appendix.......................................................................... 220

Bibliography .................................................................... 224

# Israel: The Last Vestige of European Colonialism in the Middle East

A.A. Castor

# Dedication

To my beloved family,

Your unconditional love, unwavering support, and endless encouragement have been my greatest blessings. From the earliest days of dreaming to the challenging moments of writing, you have stood by me with patience and belief. This book is as much yours as it is mine, a reflection of the values you've instilled and the faith you've shown in me. Thank you for being my rock and my inspiration.

To my dear friends,

Your friendship has illuminated my path with laughter, shared moments, and invaluable support. You've cheered me on through every triumph and lifted me up through every challenge. Your belief in my endeavors has been a source of strength and motivation. This book is a testament to the power of friendship, and I am grateful for each of you who has walked this journey by my side.

To God,

Your grace and guidance have been my constant companions. In moments of doubt, you've shown me the way; in moments of joy, you've multiplied my gratitude. This book is a testament to your faithfulness and the blessings you've bestowed upon me. May it serve as a reflection of your love and the lessons you continue to teach me.

With heartfelt gratitude and love,

A.A. Castor

# Copyright © 2024 by A.A. Castor

**Philippine Copyright Law:**

The Intellectual Property Code of the Philippines (Republic Act No. 8293) provides protection to literary and artistic works from the moment of their creation. It includes provisions for the rights of authors and copyright owners, including the exclusive right to reproduce, distribute, perform, and display their works. Unauthorized use or reproduction of copyrighted materials is subject to legal penalties under this law.

---

1.    http://www.tonyc.info

# Why I Am Writing This Book

The motivation behind writing this book lies in the need to challenge prevailing narratives and confront uncomfortable truths about the history and ongoing dynamics of Israel in the Middle East. The formation of Israel and its continued existence as a state is often framed as a triumph of the Jewish people returning to their ancestral homeland. However, this narrative conveniently overlooks the colonial elements of Israel's establishment, the displacement of indigenous Palestinians, and the role of Western powers in perpetuating inequality and injustice in the region.

This book aims to provide a critical examination of Israel as the last vestige of European colonialism in the Middle East. By exploring the historical and genetic evidence of European involvement and the consequences for Palestinians, I want to shed light on the realities that have been marginalized or outright ignored by mainstream discourse. The stories of those who were displaced, the narratives of those whose voices have been silenced, and the evidence of systemic discrimination must be brought to the forefront if we are to understand the complexities of the conflict.

I am writing this book to challenge the myth that Israel's existence is purely about the "return" of a people to their homeland. The reality is far more complex—rooted in a history of colonial interests, Western political motivations, and a disregard for the rights of the indigenous population. The perspective that Israel has an inherent right to occupy and control the land must be questioned, particularly when considering the countless injustices suffered by the Palestinians who continue to live under occupation and oppression.

Furthermore, I want to address the role of international powers in supporting Israel despite its violations of international law. The influence of Western countries—through diplomatic backing, financial aid, and military support—has ensured that Israel can continue its policies without accountability. This support reflects the ongoing impact of colonial legacies, where powerful nations continue to impose their will on vulnerable populations without facing consequences.

This book is an attempt to encourage readers to think critically about the history and present-day reality of Israel and Palestine. It is a call to action for those who believe in justice, equality, and the right of all people to live free from oppression. By confronting the colonial underpinnings of Israel's establishment and its impact on the Palestinian people, I hope to contribute to a broader understanding of the conflict and inspire meaningful dialogue about the path forward.

# Warning and Disclaimer

This book presents a critical perspective on the history and current dynamics of Israel and its relationship with Palestine. The content herein is intended to challenge mainstream narratives and explore uncomfortable truths regarding colonialism, displacement, and systemic discrimination. Readers should be aware that the views expressed may diverge significantly from widely accepted historical and political positions, particularly those that depict Israel solely as a rightful homeland for the Jewish people without addressing the impact on the indigenous Palestinian population.

The information, opinions, and analyses provided in this book are based on historical records, academic research, and interpretations of events that may be controversial or sensitive. While every effort has been made to ensure accuracy, this book does not claim to present an exhaustive account of the Israeli-Palestinian conflict. Historical events are complex, and different perspectives exist; readers are encouraged to consult multiple sources to gain a more comprehensive understanding of the subject.

The author does not advocate for hate, discrimination, or violence against any group. This book is a scholarly work aimed at raising awareness and promoting critical discussion regarding colonialism, human rights, and international law. The goal is to shed light on issues that are often overlooked or marginalized and to encourage readers to think deeply about the implications of history on current events.

The content of this book is for informational and educational purposes only. It is not intended to provide legal, political, or professional advice. Readers should seek the counsel of qualified professionals if they require guidance on specific legal or political matters related to the topics discussed.

The opinions expressed are solely those of the author and do not represent the views of any organization or entity with which the author may be affiliated. Neither the author nor the publisher shall have any liability or responsibility to any person or entity for any loss, damage, or adverse consequences alleged to have happened, directly or indirectly, as a result of the use or interpretation of the information contained in this book.

# About the Author

A.A. Castor is a dedicated writer and researcher with a deep passion for exploring the intersection of history, leadership, and social dynamics. His work focuses on uncovering historical truths, questioning established narratives, and examining the legacies of colonialism that continue to shape the modern world. With a particular interest in controversial and complex topics, Castor strives to present perspectives that challenge the status quo and provoke meaningful discussions about justice, equality, and power.

Drawing inspiration from historical figures and events, A.A. Castor's writings delve into the often-overlooked aspects of history, providing readers with a deeper understanding of how the past influences the present. His works explore themes such as political strategy, social cohesion, and the impact of propaganda on public perception, offering insights that are both thought-provoking and relevant to contemporary issues.

In addition to his work as an author, A.A. Castor is an avid podcaster, sharing his thoughts on leadership, history, and social philosophy. His research spans a wide range of topics, from political power and governance to the intricacies of human relationships. Castor's goal is to use his writing and research to engage readers in critical thinking and encourage them to question conventional wisdom, ultimately empowering them to contribute to a more just and equitable world.

# Introduction: Unveiling Colonial Roots

The formation of modern Israel is a narrative often wrapped in historical justifications, biblical claims, and nationalist zeal. However, beneath these layers lies a significant but often overlooked reality—the establishment of Israel is deeply connected to European colonialism. From the early influences of Zionist leaders inspired by European nationalist movements to the direct role of European powers in its creation, Israel's foundation fits into the broader context of colonial ventures.

European colonialism, with its defining traits of territorial expansion, settler implantation, and the marginalization of indigenous populations, has left an indelible mark on history. In the case of Israel, this colonial framework manifests in ways that mirror past European exploits in Africa, Asia, and the Americas. The European influence on Zionism, the migration of European Jews to the Middle East, and the subsequent displacement of native populations all point towards the colonial characteristics present in Israel's formation.

This book aims to uncover these European roots, challenging the popular narratives that paint the establishment of Israel as a purely biblical "return" to an ancestral homeland. By reevaluating historical, cultural, and genetic evidence, the book sheds light on the true nature of this nation's origin—one driven by the influence and interests of European powers.

Throughout the chapters, the themes of European involvement and colonial dynamics will be explored, alongside the marginalization and exclusion of the native Palestinian population. Additionally, the support provided by Western powers—financial, political, and military—will be scrutinized to understand its role in sustaining Israel's colonial legacy and the broader implications for the Middle East.

The political and financial backing from Western nations, particularly the United States and major European powers, played a decisive role in shaping Israel's status in the region. Historical motivations for this support, including strategic alliances and economic interests, have had lasting consequences on the stability and political dynamics of the Middle East. By examining these aspects, this book provides a comprehensive understanding of Israel's colonial roots and how Western powers have continued to influence its development and position in the region.

# Defining European Colonialism in the Context of Israel

### HISTORICAL COLONIALISM vs. Modern Examples

European colonialism, historically, was characterized by the expansion of European powers into foreign lands, often marked by the establishment of settler colonies, exploitation of resources, and the subjugation or displacement of native populations. Examples such as the British colonization of India, French expansion into North Africa, and the Dutch in Indonesia illustrate the traditional model of colonialism: a foreign power controlling a region for its own benefit, often to extract wealth, extend influence, and expand territories.

In contrast, modern examples of colonialism are often subtler, involving ideological control, settler expansion without direct colonial rule, and neo-colonial economic dominance. The establishment of Israel shares several similarities with traditional colonialism but also bears distinctive modern elements. Unlike historical empires, which were state-driven and overt, the colonization of Palestine was influenced by a combination of Zionist aspirations, European powers seeking influence in the Middle East, and later the geopolitical interests of Western allies. These dynamics reflect a form of modern colonialism where the influence was exerted not only through territorial conquest but through ideology, settlement, and international political support.

**Colonial Characteristics in Israel's Formation**

The formation of Israel can be examined through the lens of colonial characteristics that define traditional European colonialism. First, the migration of European Jews to Palestine was, in many ways, analogous to the settler movements seen in historical colonial enterprises. Settler colonialism is characterized by the movement of a significant number of settlers into a territory to establish control, leading to the displacement of the indigenous population. The Zionist movement encouraged Jewish migration to the region, largely driven by European Jews who were seeking refuge, driven by nationalist aspirations, and fueled by colonial ideologies of "civilizing" or "reclaiming" land.

Another colonial characteristic seen in Israel's formation is the active support of European powers, such as Britain, whose involvement was instrumental in facilitating Jewish settlement in Palestine. The Balfour Declaration of 1917 is a prime example of European political backing aimed at establishing a Jewish homeland, despite the existing Arab population's wishes. This political endorsement, followed by the British mandate, essentially laid the groundwork for a European-backed colonial endeavor, facilitating land purchases, settlement building, and ultimately the establishment of Israel.

Furthermore, the creation of Israel involved the marginalization and displacement of indigenous populations, echoing the practices seen in historical colonial projects. The displacement of Palestinians during and after the 1948 Arab-Israeli War mirrors the displacement of native populations in colonial territories, where settlers claimed land and marginalized those who originally inhabited it. The idea of "a land without a people for a people without a land"—often propagated by early Zionist rhetoric—reinforced a colonial mindset that sought to justify the settlement of land under the guise of modernization or rightful return.

The ongoing support of Israel by Western powers, particularly the United States and European countries, also reflects the economic and political interests typically seen in colonial relationships. Western nations continue to provide significant financial aid and political backing to Israel, mirroring the economic dependencies and protective relationships that defined many colonial ventures. This support ensures that Israel maintains a dominant position in the region, sustaining a form of neo-colonial influence that aligns with broader Western geopolitical interests.

These elements—the settlement of European Jews, the support of European powers, and the displacement of indigenous people—highlight the colonial characteristics inherent in the establishment of Israel. While the context and justifications differ from traditional European empires, the underlying processes share striking similarities, positioning modern Israel within the framework of European colonialism in the Middle East.

# Uncovering the European Roots of Modern Israel

**CHALLENGING COMMON Narratives About Israel's Origins**

The mainstream narrative surrounding the formation of modern Israel is often presented as the fulfillment of a historical and biblical promise—the return of the Jewish people to their ancestral homeland. This perspective has been perpetuated by religious, political, and cultural forces that emphasize a deep historical connection between the Jewish people and the land of Israel. The establishment of Israel is frequently portrayed as a natural culmination of a two-thousand-year-old yearning to return, rooted in religious texts and Jewish collective memory.

However, this narrative glosses over crucial historical and political contexts that reveal a different story—one heavily influenced by European colonialism, migration, and geopolitics. The narrative of a natural return obscures the significant role played by European powers, who supported and facilitated the Zionist movement for their own strategic purposes in the Middle East. It also ignores the impact of this project on the indigenous Palestinian population, whose displacement and marginalization were justified under the guise of biblical destiny and civilizational advancement.

This book aims to challenge these common narratives, bringing to light the colonial aspects of Israel's establishment. By questioning the myth of the "return to an empty land" and examining the broader geopolitical interests of the time, it becomes evident that the creation of Israel was not merely a spiritual or historical inevitability but rather a complex political endeavor deeply tied to European interests and colonial strategies.

### A Reevaluation of Historical, Cultural, and Genetic Evidence

To uncover the European roots of modern Israel, this book delves into historical, cultural, and genetic evidence that challenges traditional accounts. From the origins of the Zionist movement in 19th century Europe to the political maneuvers that led to the creation of the state of Israel, the historical record reveals a story deeply embedded in European colonialism. Zionism emerged as a nationalistic response to the persecution of Jews in Europe, influenced by the rise of European nationalist ideologies and shaped by a desire to create a Jewish state modeled after European nations.

The cultural influence of Europe is also evident in the formation of Israeli society. The early leaders of the Zionist movement, many of whom were European Jews, sought to create a state that mirrored European cultural values, social norms, and political structures. This cultural foundation led to a society that, while geographically situated in the Middle East, has often aligned itself more closely with Western ideologies than with its neighboring countries. The preference for European cultural models also contributed to the marginalization of non-European Jewish communities, such as Mizrahi and Sephardic Jews, who faced discrimination and exclusion in the new state.

Genetic evidence further complicates the narrative of a direct ancestral return. Studies on the genetic origins of modern Israeli Jews indicate that a significant portion of the population descends from European Ashkenazi Jews, rather than from the ancient inhabitants of the region. This evidence suggests that the establishment of Israel was less about an indigenous people reclaiming their homeland and more about a European population seeking a new territory, supported by the colonial powers of the time. The migration patterns of European Jews to Palestine in the late 19th and early 20th centuries align with the broader colonial movement of Europeans settling in new lands.

By reevaluating these aspects—historical motivations, cultural influences, and genetic evidence—this book provides a clearer understanding of the European roots of modern Israel. It highlights how the establishment of Israel fits within the broader context of European colonialism, driven by migration, settlement, and geopolitical strategy rather than the simple fulfillment of a biblical promise. The goal is to present a more nuanced perspective that acknowledges the complexities of Israel's foundation, the influence of European colonial powers, and the impact on the indigenous population, ultimately encouraging a deeper reflection on the true origins of the modern state of Israel.

# Outline of the Main Themes and Arguments

### EUROPEAN INVOLVEMENT and Colonial Framework

A central theme of this book is the role of European involvement in the establishment of modern Israel, analyzed through the lens of colonialism. The Zionist movement, which began in Europe in the late 19th century, was heavily influenced by European nationalist ideologies and colonial ambitions. Zionist leaders sought to create a Jewish homeland, and their vision was supported by key European powers such as Britain, which saw strategic opportunities in the Middle East.

The British Mandate in Palestine played a pivotal role in laying the foundation for what can be seen as a colonial project. Through policies that facilitated Jewish immigration and land acquisition, the British effectively enabled the creation of a settler society reminiscent of other European colonial endeavors. This support for the Zionist movement was not driven purely by altruism but by geopolitical motivations, such as securing a loyal ally in a strategically important region. By examining these historical contexts, it becomes evident that the formation of Israel fits within the broader colonial framework that European powers implemented in various parts of the world during the 19th and 20th centuries.

**Marginalization and Exclusion of Indigenous Populations**

Another key theme explored in this book is the marginalization and exclusion of the indigenous populations of Palestine. The establishment of Israel involved the displacement of native Palestinians, who had lived in the region for centuries. This displacement is a defining feature of colonialism, where indigenous populations are often marginalized or expelled to make way for settler communities. The 1948 Nakba, during which hundreds of thousands of Palestinians were displaced, is a stark example of this colonial characteristic.

The exclusion did not end with displacement. Within Israeli society, the indigenous Palestinian population has faced systemic discrimination and limited rights compared to Jewish citizens. This exclusion also extends to non-European Jewish communities, such as Mizrahi and Sephardic Jews, who have historically faced social and economic marginalization in a state dominated by

European-Ashkenazi culture and leadership. The colonial mindset of superiority, which was prevalent in European colonies around the world, manifests itself in the treatment of these marginalized groups, creating a hierarchy that favors European-descended individuals over others.

**Western Powers' Influence and Its Implications**

The influence of Western powers, particularly the United States and European countries, is another major theme that underpins the arguments presented in this book. From the inception of Israel to the present day, Western powers have played a significant role in shaping the political, economic, and military landscape of the region. This influence has had far-reaching implications for both the stability of the Middle East and the international perception of Israel.

The unwavering political and financial support provided by Western nations, especially the United States, has bolstered Israel's position in the region. This includes using veto power at the United Nations to shield Israel from international condemnation, providing substantial financial aid, and supplying advanced military technology. Such support not only underscores the colonial legacy but also ensures the continued dominance of Israel over its neighbors, effectively maintaining a power imbalance reminiscent of colonial protectorates. The implications of this support are profound, as they contribute to ongoing conflicts, hinder peace efforts, and perpetuate a cycle of violence and resentment in the region.

By exploring these main themes—European involvement, the marginalization of indigenous populations, and Western influence—the book aims to provide a comprehensive understanding of how Israel's foundation and continued existence are tied to colonial dynamics. These themes serve as the foundation for analyzing the true origins and nature of modern Israel, challenging prevailing narratives and offering new insights into the consequences of colonialism in the Middle East.

# The Influence of Western Powers: Political and Financial Backing of Israel

## HISTORICAL WESTERN Support and Its Motivations

The support of Western powers has been a defining factor in the establishment and sustainability of the modern state of Israel. From the early 20th century, Western nations, particularly Britain and later the United States, played instrumental roles in facilitating the creation of a Jewish homeland in Palestine. The British government's issuance of the Balfour Declaration in 1917 marked the beginning of formal Western endorsement of Zionist ambitions, laying the political groundwork for the establishment of Israel. British support during the mandate period included facilitating Jewish immigration to Palestine and allowing Zionist institutions to grow, effectively favoring Jewish settlers over the indigenous Arab population.

The motivations behind Western support for the establishment of Israel were complex and multifaceted. For Britain, maintaining influence in the strategically vital Middle East was crucial, especially given the proximity to the Suez Canal and the oil-rich Gulf region. Supporting a Jewish homeland aligned with Britain's geopolitical interests, ensuring a foothold in a region of great strategic importance. Additionally, Western nations were influenced by a sense of guilt and responsibility following the atrocities of the Holocaust, which further fueled their backing of a Jewish state. However, this support often overlooked the rights and aspirations of the indigenous Palestinian population, leading to long-term regional tensions.

As the geopolitical landscape shifted after World War II, the United States emerged as Israel's primary benefactor. American motivations were influenced by a combination of Cold War dynamics, the desire to maintain a strong ally in the Middle East, and domestic political considerations, including the influence of pro-Israel lobbying groups. For the United States, Israel became a crucial partner in countering Soviet influence in the region, serving as a reliable ally in a region where many nations were aligned with or sympathetic to the Soviet Union.

## Economic and Political Consequences for the Region

The extensive political and financial backing of Israel by Western powers has had profound economic and political consequences for the Middle East. One of the most significant outcomes has been the entrenchment of Israel's military dominance in the region. The substantial military aid provided by the United States, including advanced weaponry and technology, has ensured that Israel maintains a qualitative military edge over its neighbors. This military advantage has allowed Israel to carry out operations in neighboring territories with relative impunity, often leading to increased tensions and cycles of violence that have destabilized the region.

Financial support from Western nations, particularly the United States, has also played a key role in bolstering Israel's economy, enabling the country to develop advanced infrastructure, technology, and defense industries. This economic backing has contributed to the disparity between Israel and its neighboring countries, many of which struggle with economic challenges and lack similar levels of international support. The economic imbalance has fueled resentment among neighboring Arab nations and has been a source of ongoing friction, as Israel's prosperity is often viewed in stark contrast to the economic hardships faced by Palestinians and other regional populations.

Politically, the unwavering support of Western powers for Israel has had significant repercussions for international diplomacy in the Middle East. The use of veto power by the United States at the United Nations to block resolutions critical of Israel has undermined efforts to hold Israel accountable for its actions, including settlement expansion and human rights violations. This has contributed to a perception of double standards in the application of international law, eroding trust in global institutions and diminishing the credibility of Western nations as impartial brokers in the peace process.

The political backing of Israel by Western powers has also isolated the Palestinian people, limiting their ability to achieve self-determination. Western nations' consistent alignment with Israel has marginalized Palestinian voices in international forums, reducing their bargaining power and perpetuating the status quo of occupation and limited autonomy. This has not only hindered the prospects for a peaceful resolution to the Israeli-Palestinian conflict but has also fueled extremism and radicalization, as disenfranchised populations turn to more militant means to achieve their goals in the absence of meaningful diplomatic progress.

The influence of Western powers—through political endorsement, financial aid, and military support—has thus played a crucial role in shaping the dynamics of the Israeli-Palestinian conflict and the broader Middle East. This support has ensured Israel's security and prosperity but has also come at a significant cost to regional stability, contributing to cycles of conflict, economic disparities, and political tensions that continue to affect the region to this day. By examining these aspects, it becomes clear that the Western backing of Israel is not just a historical artifact but an ongoing influence with far-reaching consequences.

# Chapter 1: Historical Background of Zionism and European

Chapter 1 delves into the historical roots of Zionism and the significant role played by European powers in shaping the path to the establishment of Israel. The story of Zionism cannot be separated from the broader political and social movements of 19th century Europe, which laid the foundation for nationalist ideologies across the continent. During this time, as nationalism surged, many European Jews began envisioning a homeland of their own—an idea that gave rise to the modern Zionist movement. The political climate, characterized by rising national aspirations and social transformations, profoundly influenced the leaders of early Zionism, who sought to create a nation-state for Jews based on the European model of nationalism.

Key figures like Theodor Herzl and Chaim Weizmann emerged from the backdrop of European intellectual circles, embodying the philosophies and nationalist ideals that were gaining traction across the continent. Their vision for a Jewish homeland was shaped by the European experience of national self-determination and the desire to create a state modeled after European nations, with its own institutions and governance. The early leaders of the Zionist movement were driven by a combination of responding to anti-Semitism in Europe and adopting the prevailing ideas of statehood and national unity that defined 19th and early 20th century Europe.

The role of European powers, particularly Britain, was instrumental in turning the Zionist dream into a political reality. British interests in the Middle East were primarily strategic—maintaining control over trade routes and establishing influence in a geopolitically significant region. This led to Britain's pivotal support of the Zionist cause, notably through the Balfour Declaration of 1917, which expressed support for the establishment of a "national home for the Jewish people" in Palestine. The subsequent British Mandate period provided the institutional framework that enabled Jewish immigration and settlement, laying the groundwork for the eventual creation of the state of Israel.

The involvement of other European powers, including France and Germany, also played a part, though often in complex and sometimes conflicting ways. Their support, motivations, and tensions influenced the Zionist movement and its progress toward statehood. During the British Mandate, policies regarding land, governance, and local populations set the stage for future conflicts, while diplomacy during the interwar period highlighted the challenges of establishing a European-backed state in a predominantly Arab region.

Chapter 1 provides a comprehensive examination of these historical events, highlighting how European political interests, philosophical influences, and strategic motivations were central to the formation of Zionism and the subsequent establishment of Israel. This historical context reveals how deeply embedded European colonial dynamics were in the creation of Israel, setting the stage for the conflicts and issues that continue to shape the region today.

# The Origins of Zionism: The European Context

**POLITICAL AND SOCIAL Movements in 19th Century Europe**

The origins of modern Zionism are deeply rooted in the political and social movements that swept across Europe in the 19th century. This period was marked by significant upheavals and transformations, including the Industrial Revolution, the decline of feudal structures, and the emergence of liberal and nationalist ideologies. The rise of nationalism, in particular, played a pivotal role in shaping the aspirations of various ethnic and religious groups, including the Jews of Europe. As European nations sought to define themselves as distinct entities based on shared culture, language, and heritage, minority groups like the Jews found themselves increasingly marginalized.

The spread of nationalist ideas coincided with a surge in anti-Semitic sentiment across Europe, exacerbating the exclusion faced by Jewish communities. Pogroms in Eastern Europe, state-sanctioned discrimination, and social exclusion in Western Europe all contributed to a growing sense of urgency among Jews to find a solution to their precarious status. In this context, the Jewish question—how Jews could achieve equal rights, security, and self-determination—became a central issue, giving rise to the idea of establishing a homeland where Jews could live free from persecution.

The broader political environment of Europe, with its emphasis on self-determination and national identity, provided a model for the Jewish people. The wave of nationalist movements that led to the unification of Italy and Germany, as well as the revolutions of 1848, demonstrated the power of collective action and the possibility of creating a nation-state based on shared identity. These developments influenced Jewish intellectuals and activists, who began to advocate for the idea of a Jewish homeland—initially considering options outside of Palestine but eventually focusing on the historical land of Israel as the most fitting location.

### The Rise of Nationalism and Its Influence on Zionism

Nationalism's rise had a profound influence on the development of Zionist thought. Theodor Herzl, often regarded as the father of modern political Zionism, was directly influenced by the nationalist fervor of his time. Herzl witnessed the Dreyfus Affair in France—a stark example of how anti-Semitism persisted even in nations that prided themselves on liberty and equality. The realization that assimilation was not a viable solution for European Jews led Herzl and other leaders to conclude that the only way to ensure Jewish safety and self-determination was through the establishment of a sovereign Jewish state.

Zionism emerged as a nationalist movement that sought to emulate the successes of other European nationalist projects. Herzl's vision, as outlined in his seminal work "Der Judenstaat" ("The Jewish State"), was explicitly modeled on the European concept of the nation-state. He called for the establishment of a Jewish homeland where Jews could govern themselves and live without fear of persecution, much like other peoples in Europe who were striving for national independence. Herzl's efforts culminated in the convening of the First Zionist Congress in Basel in 1897, where the goal of establishing a Jewish homeland in Palestine was formally articulated.

The rise of nationalism also influenced the cultural aspects of Zionism, as the movement sought to create a unified Jewish identity that transcended the diverse cultural backgrounds of Jews living across Europe and beyond. This included the revival of Hebrew as a spoken language, the promotion of a distinct Jewish culture, and the emphasis on a shared historical and religious connection to the land of Israel. These cultural elements were essential in fostering a sense of unity and purpose among Jews, many of whom had lived in diaspora communities for centuries with varying degrees of assimilation into their host societies.

Zionism, therefore, can be seen as both a response to the political and social challenges faced by Jews in 19th century Europe and an adoption of the nationalist principles that were reshaping the continent. It was a movement that sought to secure a place for Jews in a world that was increasingly defined by national borders and ethnic identities. By drawing on the European experience of nation-building, Zionist leaders aimed to create a state where Jews could achieve the same rights, security, and sense of belonging that other national groups in Europe were fighting for. This European context was crucial in shaping the ideological foundations of Zionism and ultimately in the pursuit of a Jewish homeland in Palestine.

# Early Zionist Leaders and Their European Influence

**KEY FIGURES: THEODOR Herzl, Chaim Weizmann, and Others**

The early leaders of the Zionist movement were profoundly shaped by their European upbringing, education, and exposure to the political currents of their time. Theodor Herzl, often considered the father of modern political Zionism, was a Viennese journalist who witnessed firsthand the pervasive anti-Semitism in Europe, especially during the Dreyfus Affair in France. The Dreyfus Affair, in which a Jewish French military officer was wrongfully accused of treason, highlighted the fragility of Jewish rights and the persistence of deep-seated prejudice even in societies that were ostensibly committed to liberty and equality. Herzl concluded that the only solution for the Jewish people was the establishment of a state of their own, where they could control their destiny and live free from persecution.

Herzl's vision for a Jewish homeland was fundamentally influenced by the nationalist ideologies sweeping across Europe. He believed that the Jewish people, like other nations seeking self-determination, had a right to establish their own state. His book, "Der Judenstaat" ("The Jewish State"), published in 1896, laid out a practical plan for the establishment of such a state, and his efforts culminated in the organization of the First Zionist Congress in Basel in 1897. Herzl's ability to galvanize support among Jews in Europe and to gain the attention of influential political figures was a testament to his understanding of European political systems and his skill in navigating them.

Chaim Weizmann, another key figure in the Zionist movement, played an instrumental role in garnering British support for the establishment of a Jewish homeland. Weizmann, a chemist by training, moved in elite circles in Britain and used his connections to advance the Zionist cause. His efforts culminated in the issuance of the Balfour Declaration in 1917, in which the British government expressed support for "the establishment in Palestine of a national home for the Jewish people." Weizmann's diplomatic acumen and his ability to appeal to British strategic interests were crucial in securing this support, demonstrating the importance of European political influence in the realization of Zionist goals.

Other prominent figures, such as Max Nordau and Ze'ev Jabotinsky, also played significant roles in shaping the Zionist movement. Nordau, a close collaborator of Herzl, was a physician and social critic who used his platform to advocate for the necessity of a Jewish state. Jabotinsky, influenced by the rising tide of European nationalism, founded the Revisionist Zionist movement, which emphasized the need for a strong, militaristic approach to securing Jewish statehood. Each of these leaders brought their unique perspectives, shaped by their European experiences, to the movement, contributing to the diverse ideological foundation of Zionism.

**European Philosophies Embedded in Zionist Thought**

The early Zionist leaders were deeply influenced by the philosophical and ideological currents of 19th and early 20th century Europe. Nationalism was perhaps the most significant influence, as it provided the framework for Zionism's central goal: the creation of a sovereign Jewish state. In the wake of the nationalist movements that led to the unification of Italy and Germany, Zionist leaders adopted the idea that Jews, too, constituted a distinct nation deserving of self-determination. This concept of nationalism was not merely about establishing a state but also about fostering a collective identity, culture, and language—a vision that was embodied in the revival of Hebrew as a spoken language and in the emphasis on a shared Jewish history.

Herzl's political Zionism was also influenced by European liberalism, which advocated for the rights of individuals and national groups to self-determination. Herzl believed that the Jewish people had a natural right to establish their own state, just as other national groups in Europe were doing. His writings reflect a belief in the liberal ideals of equality and freedom, though he also recognized that these ideals were often denied to Jews in European societies. Herzl's vision of a Jewish state was one that would be modern, secular, and democratic, modeled on the liberal European states of his time.

Socialist ideas also played a significant role in shaping Zionist thought, particularly among leaders like Ber Borochov and later David Ben-Gurion. Labor Zionism, a branch of the movement that emphasized the importance of building a socialist society in Palestine, was influenced by the socialist and labor movements that were gaining momentum in Europe. The idea was that the Jewish state should not only be a refuge for persecuted Jews but also a society built on principles of social justice and equality. This led to the establishment of collective agricultural communities known as kibbutzim, which became a defining feature of early Jewish settlement in Palestine.

At the same time, elements of European colonial thought were also embedded in Zionism. The idea of "making the desert bloom" and bringing modern civilization to what was perceived as an underdeveloped land was reminiscent of the civilizing mission that underpinned European colonial ventures. This aspect of Zionist ideology reflected a belief in the superiority of European culture and the notion that European Jews were bringing progress to Palestine, often ignoring or dismissing the presence and rights of the indigenous Arab population.

The blend of nationalism, liberalism, socialism, and colonial attitudes formed the ideological bedrock of early Zionism, influencing both the goals of the movement and the methods employed to achieve them. These European philosophies not only shaped the vision of a Jewish state but also defined the relationship between the Jewish settlers and the native inhabitants of Palestine, setting the stage for the conflicts that would follow. By understanding the European influences on early Zionist leaders and their ideologies, one gains a clearer picture of how the movement evolved and the challenges it faced in the pursuit of its goals.

# The Role of British and Other European Powers in Establishing Israel

**BRITISH INTERESTS IN the Middle East: Strategic Objectives**

The British played a central role in the establishment of the state of Israel, driven by a combination of strategic interests and political considerations. During World War I, Britain sought to secure its position in the Middle East, particularly as it related to maintaining control over vital trade routes such as the Suez Canal, which was a crucial link to its colonial holdings in India. The Middle East, with its emerging oil resources, was also becoming strategically important, and Britain aimed to ensure that it maintained influence over this region, especially in the face of rival powers such as France and the Ottoman Empire.

The Balfour Declaration of 1917, in which the British government expressed support for "the establishment in Palestine of a national home for the Jewish people," was a key moment in the formal backing of the Zionist movement. The declaration was not simply an altruistic gesture towards the Jewish people but a calculated move that aligned with British strategic objectives. By supporting the establishment of a Jewish homeland in Palestine, Britain hoped to secure the support of the Jewish community, both within the British Empire and in the United States, which was emerging as a key player on the world stage. The British also viewed a Jewish presence in Palestine as a means of securing a loyal population that could help stabilize the region and serve as a buffer against potential threats.

Following World War I, Britain was granted the Mandate for Palestine by the League of Nations, effectively giving it control over the territory. During the mandate period (1920-1948), British policies facilitated the growth of the Jewish community in Palestine, including the promotion of Jewish immigration and land acquisition. While the

British attempted to balance the interests of both Jewish and Arab populations, their policies often favored the Zionist cause, leading to increased tensions and outbreaks of violence. The infrastructure and administrative frameworks established during the British Mandate laid the groundwork for the eventual creation of the state of Israel, as Jewish institutions such as the Jewish Agency and the Haganah (a paramilitary organization) developed under British oversight.

**France, Germany, and Other European Powers: Support and Tensions**

While Britain played the most direct role in the establishment of Israel, other European powers also influenced the course of Zionism and the eventual founding of the state. France, for instance, had its own interests in the Middle East, particularly in Syria and Lebanon, which were under French mandate. The relationship between France and the Zionist movement was complex, with France at times offering support to the Jews, particularly in the wake of the Holocaust. During the 1940s, French support for the Zionist underground movement grew, partly as a way to counter British influence in the region. This rivalry between colonial powers meant that France saw an opportunity in supporting Jewish aspirations, especially as the British faced increasing resistance in Palestine.

Germany's role in the Zionist story is more complicated and varied over time. Before the rise of the Nazis, Germany had a significant Jewish population, and many German Jews were active in the Zionist movement. However, with the rise of Hitler and the implementation of anti-Semitic policies, many German Jews fled to Palestine, significantly boosting the Jewish population there and lending urgency to the Zionist cause. Ironically, the persecution of Jews in Europe by Nazi Germany accelerated the very movement that would lead to the establishment of Israel.

Other European countries also had varying degrees of influence on the Zionist movement. Russia, for instance, was home to a large Jewish population that faced severe persecution in the form of pogroms, driving many Jews to emigrate to Palestine. The early Zionist movement drew significant support from Russian Jews, many of whom brought with them socialist ideals that influenced the development of Labor Zionism and the establishment of kibbutzim, collective agricultural communities in Palestine. Eastern European Jews, in general, formed the backbone of the early waves of Jewish migration to Palestine, driven by both Zionist ideals and the harsh realities of life in Europe.

Throughout this period, the tensions between the various European powers—Britain, France, Germany, and Russia—shaped the environment in which the Zionist movement operated. The rivalry between Britain and France, in particular, had a direct impact on the Middle East, as each sought to expand its influence in the region. This competition sometimes worked to the advantage of the Zionist movement, as the Jewish leaders were able to garner support from different powers at different times, depending on the shifting political landscape.

The involvement of European powers in the establishment of Israel was thus marked by a combination of strategic objectives, political rivalries, and responses to the evolving situation in Europe. While Britain provided the most direct support through the Balfour Declaration and the Mandate for Palestine, the roles of France, Germany, Russia, and other European countries also significantly shaped the trajectory of Zionism. Their support, motivations, and at times conflicting interests contributed to the complexities of establishing a Jewish homeland in Palestine, setting the stage for the conflicts and alliances that would define the region in the decades to come.

# The Balfour Declaration and British Mandate: Laying the Groundwork for a European Colony

## BRITISH MANDATE POLICIES and Their Impact on Local Populations

The Balfour Declaration of 1917 was a critical moment in the history of Zionism and the eventual establishment of Israel. It was a formal statement from the British government that expressed support for "the establishment in Palestine of a national home for the Jewish people." This declaration was not a legally binding document, but it carried significant political weight, given Britain's emerging influence in the region as World War I drew to a close. The declaration was driven by a combination of strategic interests, including securing Jewish support during the war, creating a stable ally in the Middle East, and countering the influence of other colonial powers.

Following the end of World War I, the League of Nations granted Britain the Mandate for Palestine, effectively giving it administrative control over the territory. The mandate period, which lasted from 1920 to 1948, was characterized by British efforts to implement the goals of the Balfour Declaration while simultaneously trying to manage the conflicting interests of the Jewish and Arab populations. British mandate policies were instrumental in laying the foundation for the creation of a Jewish homeland, but they also sowed the seeds of future conflict.

Under the mandate, Britain facilitated Jewish immigration to Palestine, allowing for the steady growth of the Jewish population. This was particularly significant during the 1930s, when Jews fleeing persecution in Europe sought refuge in Palestine. British policies also enabled Jewish land acquisition, which led to the establishment of agricultural settlements and urban development by the Jewish community. These policies were aligned with the goals of the Zionist movement, which sought to build the infrastructure necessary for a future state. The establishment of institutions such as the Jewish Agency and the Haganah (a Jewish paramilitary organization) further strengthened the Jewish community's ability to govern itself and defend its interests.

However, these policies had a significant impact on the local Arab population. Palestinian Arabs, who had lived in the region for centuries, found themselves increasingly marginalized as Jewish immigration and land purchases altered the demographic and economic landscape. The displacement of Palestinian farmers from land sold to Jewish settlers led to widespread resentment and anger, which was further exacerbated by the perception that the British were favoring the Zionist cause. The growth of Jewish settlements and the increasing influence of the Jewish community led to tensions and outbreaks of violence, including the Arab revolts of 1920, 1929, and 1936-1939, which were brutally suppressed by the British.

The British also imposed a dual system of governance, which effectively divided the population along ethnic lines. The Jewish community was allowed to develop its own institutions and operate semi-autonomously, while the Arab population was largely excluded from similar opportunities. This divide-and-rule approach, reminiscent of other colonial ventures, served to deepen the divisions between the two communities, making it increasingly difficult to find common ground. The legacy of these policies is still felt today, as the seeds of conflict sown during the mandate period continue to shape the Israeli-Palestinian conflict.

## Conflict and Diplomacy During the Interwar Period

The interwar period was marked by a series of conflicts and diplomatic maneuvers that reflected the growing tensions in Palestine and the broader geopolitical interests of Britain and other European powers. As Jewish immigration increased, so too did the resistance from the local Arab population, which feared losing its land and political rights. The British, caught between their commitment to the Balfour Declaration and the need to maintain order, found themselves increasingly unable to satisfy either side.

The 1920s and 1930s saw numerous instances of violence between Jewish and Arab communities, often sparked by disputes over land, immigration, and political representation. In response to these tensions, the British issued a series of White Papers—policy statements aimed at clarifying their position and attempting to manage the conflicting demands of the two communities. The 1930 Passfield White Paper, for instance, sought to limit Jewish immigration and land purchases, but it faced strong opposition from the Zionist movement, which saw it as a betrayal of the promises made in the Balfour Declaration. The 1939 White Paper, issued in response to the Arab revolt of 1936-1939, went even further, restricting Jewish immigration and land purchases in an effort to placate the Arab population and maintain stability on the eve of World War II.

These policy shifts reflected Britain's struggle to balance its strategic interests with the realities on the ground. On the one hand, Britain needed to maintain stability in Palestine to protect its broader interests in the Middle East, including access to oil and control of key trade routes. On the other hand, it faced pressure from both the Zionist movement, which had strong support in Britain and the United States, and the Arab population, which was increasingly vocal in its demands for independence and resistance to Jewish immigration.

The diplomatic maneuvering during the interwar period also involved other European powers. France, which held the mandate for Syria and Lebanon, was closely watching developments in Palestine, as any instability could spill over into its own territories. The rivalry between Britain and France, both of whom sought to expand their influence in the region, added another layer of complexity to the situation. Germany, under Nazi rule, contributed to the tensions by driving thousands of Jews to seek refuge in Palestine, further exacerbating the demographic changes and the fears of the Arab population.

By the end of the mandate period, it had become clear that Britain could no longer manage the conflicting demands of the Jewish and Arab populations. The rise of militant groups on both sides, the intensification of violence, and the growing international pressure forced Britain to announce its intention to withdraw from Palestine in 1947, leaving the future of the territory in the hands of the newly formed United Nations. The groundwork laid during the mandate period, with its emphasis on facilitating Jewish settlement and marginalizing the local Arab population, set the stage for the partition of Palestine and the creation of the state of Israel, which would be declared in 1948.

The Balfour Declaration and British Mandate thus played a crucial role in establishing the conditions for a European-style colony in Palestine. British policies, motivated by strategic interests and influenced by colonial attitudes, facilitated the growth of the Jewish community while marginalizing the indigenous Arab population, creating a legacy of division and conflict that continues to shape the region today. The interwar period, marked by violence and diplomatic maneuvering, highlighted the inherent contradictions in Britain's promises and its inability to reconcile the conflicting aspirations of the Jewish and Arab populations.

# Chapter 2: Migration Patterns and Genetic Evidence

Chapter 2 explores the migration patterns of European Jews to Palestine and the genetic evidence that reveals the origins of modern Israeli society. The migration of European Jews to Palestine took place in multiple waves, each driven by distinct social, political, and historical factors. These migration phases, beginning in the late 19th century and continuing into the post-Holocaust era, played a crucial role in shaping the demographics of what would become the state of Israel. The early waves of migration, spurred by Zionist ideals and escaping persecution in Europe, laid the foundation for the creation of a Jewish homeland, while the influx of Holocaust survivors after World War II solidified the Jewish presence in the region, eventually leading to the establishment of the state of Israel in 1948.

Genetic studies provide further insight into the origins of modern Israelis, revealing a significant European ancestry within the population. This evidence challenges the common perception of a direct return of an indigenous population to their ancestral homeland, instead highlighting the European roots of many Jewish migrants. By examining the genetic distinctions between different Jewish groups—Ashkenazi, Mizrahi, and Sephardic Jews—this chapter aims to provide a deeper understanding of the diverse backgrounds of Israeli society and how these differences have shaped cultural and social dynamics.

A comparison between the genetic profiles of modern Israelis and the indigenous Middle Eastern and African populations reveals important distinctions that have implications for identity and belonging within Israeli society. The impact of European ancestry on social and cultural identity is evident in the ways in which European-descended Jews have often held positions of power and influence, while other groups, such as Mizrahi and African Jews, have faced marginalization.

The chapter also examines the broader impact of European migration on Israeli demographics, particularly how shifting population dynamics have influenced social policies, political power structures, and cultural identity. The legacy of European migration continues to shape modern Israeli society, both in terms of its demographic makeup and the policies that govern the relationships between different communities. By understanding these migration patterns and their genetic implications, this chapter provides a comprehensive view of the European influence on the formation and evolution of Israel.

# European Jewish Migration to Israel: Historical Phases

**EARLY MIGRATION WAVES: Late 19th to Early 20th Century**

The migration of European Jews to Palestine began in earnest during the late 19th century, driven by the rise of the Zionist movement and the social and political challenges faced by Jews in Europe. The late 1800s saw a surge of nationalist movements across Europe, which inspired Zionist leaders to advocate for the establishment of a Jewish homeland in Palestine. The idea of a national revival gained traction among Jews, particularly those who were facing discrimination, pogroms, and rising anti-Semitism in Eastern Europe and Russia. These early migration waves are commonly known as the First and Second Aliyahs, referring to the Hebrew term for "ascent," signifying a return to the historical land of Israel.

The First Aliyah (1882-1903) saw a small number of Jewish migrants, primarily from Eastern Europe, who sought to escape persecution and pursue agricultural opportunities in Palestine. Many of these early settlers established agricultural colonies, hoping to cultivate the land and lay the foundation for a future Jewish state. However, the settlers faced numerous challenges, including harsh living conditions, limited resources, and conflicts with the existing Arab population. Despite these difficulties, the foundations of a Jewish presence in Palestine were laid during this period.

The Second Aliyah (1904-1914) was characterized by a more ideologically driven migration, with an influx of Jews from Russia who were motivated not only by escaping anti-Semitism but also by socialist and Zionist ideals. These settlers were determined to build a new society based on collective labor, leading to the establishment of the first kibbutzim, or collective farming communities. This wave of migration marked a significant shift in the Zionist project, with an emphasis on creating a self-sufficient Jewish society that could serve as the nucleus for a future state. The settlers of the Second Aliyah also played a crucial role in establishing key Zionist institutions and laying the groundwork for political organization, which would later become essential in the push for statehood.

**Post-Holocaust Migration and the Establishment of the State of Israel**

The next major phase of European Jewish migration to Palestine occurred in the aftermath of World War II and the Holocaust. The devastation wrought by the Holocaust, which resulted in the murder of six million Jews, created a profound sense of urgency among survivors and the broader Jewish community to establish a safe haven for Jews. The horrors of the Holocaust galvanized international support for the Zionist cause, and many European Jews, left homeless and traumatized, sought refuge in Palestine as the only viable option for rebuilding their lives.

Between 1945 and 1948, tens of thousands of Holocaust survivors made their way to Palestine, often in defiance of British immigration restrictions that were in place during the British Mandate. The British, who were attempting to maintain stability in the region, imposed limits on Jewish immigration in response to growing tensions between the Jewish and Arab populations. Despite these restrictions, Jewish refugees continued to arrive, often with the help of underground organizations that facilitated their journey. The determination of these migrants to reach Palestine, despite the risks and challenges, reflected the widespread belief that a Jewish homeland was the only way to ensure the safety and security of the Jewish people.

The influx of Holocaust survivors played a significant role in the establishment of the state of Israel in 1948. The demographic growth brought about by this migration strengthened the Jewish presence in Palestine and provided the manpower needed to defend the nascent state during the 1948 Arab-Israeli War. The establishment of Israel marked the culmination of decades of Zionist efforts and migration waves that had transformed the demographic landscape of Palestine, shifting the balance in favor of a predominantly Jewish state. The Declaration of Independence on May 14, 1948, signified not only the birth of a new nation but also the realization of the aspirations of countless European Jews who had migrated to the region over the preceding decades.

This post-Holocaust migration also set the stage for significant demographic and political changes in the region. The arrival of large numbers of European Jews and the subsequent establishment of Israel led to the displacement of hundreds of thousands of Palestinians, creating a refugee crisis that persists to this day. The legacy of these migration waves is thus intertwined with both the creation of a Jewish homeland and the enduring conflict between Israelis and Palestinians, as both peoples lay claim to the same land.

The historical phases of European Jewish migration to Israel reflect the evolving motivations and challenges faced by Jews seeking to establish a homeland. From the early agricultural pioneers of the late 19th century to the Holocaust survivors seeking refuge, these waves of migration were instrumental in shaping the foundation and character of the modern state of Israel, while also contributing to the ongoing complexities and conflicts of the region.

# Genetic Studies: Evidence of European Ancestry in Modern Israelis

## SUMMARY OF KEY GENETIC Research Studies

Genetic studies have provided significant insight into the ancestry of modern Israeli Jews, revealing a complex blend of origins that include a substantial European component. Several key studies have examined the genetic makeup of Jewish populations worldwide, with a particular focus on tracing their historical migrations and understanding how different Jewish communities are related. These studies often use DNA markers to establish genetic similarities and differences between populations, and they have revealed that Ashkenazi Jews, who make up a significant portion of the Israeli population, have a notable proportion of European ancestry.

One of the most important findings from these genetic studies is that Ashkenazi Jews, whose origins trace back to Central and Eastern Europe, carry a mix of Middle Eastern and European genetic markers. Researchers have found that while a portion of their ancestry can be linked to ancient Jewish populations from the Levant, a significant part also comes from European populations, likely due to intermarriage and conversion during the centuries that Jews lived in Europe. The genetic diversity observed among Ashkenazi Jews suggests that their ancestors included both Middle Eastern Jews who migrated to Europe and European converts to Judaism, resulting in a unique genetic profile that combines elements of both regions.

In contrast, studies of Jewish communities from the Middle East and North Africa, such as Mizrahi and Sephardic Jews, show a stronger genetic connection to the ancient populations of the Levant. These groups have remained more geographically localized and have had less intermarriage with European populations, leading to a genetic profile that more closely resembles the original Jewish populations from the region. The genetic evidence, therefore, points to significant differences in the historical experiences of these groups, with Ashkenazi Jews showing greater levels of admixture due to their centuries-long presence in Europe.

**Differences Between Ashkenazi, Mizrahi, and Sephardic Populations**

The differences in ancestry between Ashkenazi, Mizrahi, and Sephardic Jews highlight the diverse origins of modern Jewish communities and their distinct historical experiences. Ashkenazi Jews, who primarily lived in Central and Eastern Europe, have a genetic profile that reflects both their Middle Eastern origins and the influence of the European populations among whom they lived. This genetic admixture is the result of centuries of coexistence with non-Jewish Europeans, which included intermarriage and conversion. Consequently, Ashkenazi Jews tend to have genetic markers that are shared with European populations, as well as markers that trace back to the Levant.

Mizrahi Jews, who come from the Middle East, and Sephardic Jews, originally from Spain and Portugal and later dispersed throughout the Mediterranean, have a different genetic history. Mizrahi Jews have largely remained in the Middle East since ancient times, and their genetic makeup reflects a closer connection to the original Jewish populations of the region. Their genetic markers are more similar to those of other Middle Eastern populations, indicating a more continuous presence in the region with limited intermixing with European populations. Sephardic Jews, on the other hand, show some evidence of admixture with the populations of the Mediterranean and North Africa, but they also retain a strong genetic connection to their Levantine origins.

The differences between these groups have implications for understanding the cultural and social dynamics within Israeli society. The genetic diversity among Jewish populations reflects the different migration histories and levels of integration into host societies experienced by each group. Ashkenazi Jews, having lived in Europe for many centuries, brought with them not only genetic traits but also cultural influences from Europe, which have played a dominant role in shaping Israeli culture and politics. Mizrahi and Sephardic Jews, with their closer connection to Middle Eastern traditions, have faced challenges in integrating into an Israeli society that has often prioritized European cultural norms and values.

These genetic studies help to illustrate the broader historical narrative of the Jewish diaspora, highlighting the diverse origins of Jewish communities and the ways in which their distinct histories have shaped their identities. The presence of substantial European ancestry among Ashkenazi Jews complicates the narrative of a direct "return" to an ancestral homeland, as it underscores the influence of centuries of life in Europe on the genetic and cultural makeup of a significant portion of Israel's population. This diversity is both a strength and a source of tension within Israeli society, reflecting the multiple layers of identity and belonging that characterize the modern state of Israel.

# Comparison with Indigenous Middle Eastern and African Populations

**GENETIC DISTINCTIONS: Middle Eastern and African Jewish Populations**

The genetic makeup of Jewish populations that originate from the Middle East and Africa—such as Mizrahi, Sephardic, and Ethiopian Jews—offers a different perspective from that of European-descended Ashkenazi Jews. Genetic studies have shown that Mizrahi Jews, who come from countries like Iraq, Iran, Yemen, and other parts of the Middle East, share a closer genetic affinity with other indigenous populations of the region. Unlike Ashkenazi Jews, who have a significant amount of European admixture, Mizrahi Jews have largely preserved their genetic links to the ancient Jewish populations of the Levant. This continuity is evident in genetic markers that are shared with other Middle Eastern communities, suggesting that Mizrahi Jews remained geographically and genetically closer to their ancestral origins.

Similarly, Sephardic Jews, whose roots trace back to Spain and Portugal and who later migrated to North Africa and other parts of the Mediterranean, also maintain a strong genetic link to the Levant. Although they have experienced some genetic admixture with surrounding populations during their history in North Africa and the Mediterranean, their genetic profile still retains significant elements that point back to the original Jewish population of the ancient Near East. This distinguishes them from Ashkenazi Jews, who experienced more extensive genetic mixing during their time in Europe.

Ethiopian Jews, also known as Beta Israel, present a unique case. Their genetic background is distinct from both Ashkenazi and Mizrahi Jews, and they appear to have a complex ancestry that includes both ancient Jewish lineage and genetic contributions from African populations. The Beta Israel community's connection to Judaism has been historically and religiously significant, but genetically, they exhibit a different pattern compared to other Jewish groups, reflecting their long history in sub-Saharan Africa. This has led to ongoing debates regarding their origins, but genetic studies suggest a combination of African and possible ancient Jewish ancestry, indicating a unique historical path of connection to Judaism.

**The Impact of European Ancestry on Social and Cultural Identity**

The differences in genetic ancestry among Jewish communities have significant implications for social and cultural identity in modern Israel. The substantial European ancestry of Ashkenazi Jews has played a major role in shaping the cultural norms and political landscape of Israel. Ashkenazi Jews, who make up a considerable portion of the population and have historically held positions of power, brought with them the cultural values, traditions, and social practices of European societies. This has led to a dominance of European culture in Israeli society, influencing everything from the arts and education to political institutions and economic structures.

In contrast, Mizrahi, Sephardic, and Ethiopian Jews, whose genetic and cultural backgrounds are rooted in the Middle East and Africa, have often faced challenges in integrating into a society that has been shaped by European influences. The genetic distinctions between these groups are not merely biological—they also reflect the different cultural identities and historical experiences that each community brings to Israel. Mizrahi and Sephardic Jews, with their closer ties to Middle Eastern culture, have contributed significantly to the cultural mosaic of Israel, but their traditions and practices have often been marginalized in favor of those brought by European-descended Jews.

The impact of European ancestry on social identity in Israel is evident in the socioeconomic disparities that exist between different Jewish communities. Ashkenazi Jews have historically occupied more privileged positions in Israeli society, while Mizrahi, Sephardic, and Ethiopian Jews have often faced discrimination and limited opportunities. This stratification is, in part, a legacy of the cultural and historical biases that favor European heritage over other backgrounds. The cultural hegemony of European Jews has led to the marginalization of non-European traditions, creating tensions and a sense of inequality that persists to this day.

In recent years, there has been a growing movement to recognize and celebrate the diverse cultural contributions of all Jewish communities in Israel. Mizrahi and Sephardic culture, in particular, has gained greater visibility and appreciation, and efforts have been made to address the social and economic inequalities faced by these communities. However, the legacy of European ancestry and its impact on social and cultural identity continues to influence Israeli society, shaping the dynamics of inclusion, representation, and belonging.

These genetic and cultural distinctions reveal the complexity of Jewish identity in Israel, which is not monolithic but rather a tapestry of diverse histories and experiences. Understanding the genetic differences between Ashkenazi, Mizrahi, Sephardic, and Ethiopian Jews helps to illuminate the broader social dynamics within Israel, highlighting both the richness of its cultural diversity and the challenges that arise from the historical dominance of European heritage in shaping national identity.

# The Impact of European Migration on Israeli Demographics

**SHIFTING POPULATION Dynamics in the Region**

The migration of European Jews to Palestine, particularly during the late 19th and early 20th centuries, and following the Holocaust, had a profound impact on the population dynamics of the region. These waves of migration significantly increased the Jewish population in Palestine, altering the demographic balance between the Jewish and Arab communities. Prior to the large-scale arrival of European Jews, Palestine was home to a predominantly Arab population, consisting of both Muslim and Christian communities, along with a small indigenous Jewish population. However, the influx of European Jews led to a rapid growth of the Jewish community, shifting the demographics in favor of a more balanced population between Jews and Arabs by the mid-20th century.

The demographic shift accelerated in the aftermath of World War II and the Holocaust, as thousands of displaced European Jews sought refuge in Palestine. This influx not only increased the Jewish population but also created significant tension with the Arab population, which perceived the growing Jewish presence as a threat to their land, resources, and political influence. The demographic changes ultimately played a major role in the tensions that led to the 1948 Arab-Israeli War, during which many Palestinians were displaced, resulting in further demographic shifts that solidified the Jewish majority in the newly established state of Israel.

The shifting population dynamics brought about by European migration have also led to significant changes in the region's social and cultural landscape. European Jews brought with them the customs, languages, and traditions of their countries of origin, which influenced the developing culture of Israel. Hebrew, which had been largely a liturgical language, was revived and modernized, becoming the official language of the new state. European social and political ideologies, such as socialism, also played a key role in shaping the early political institutions and social structures of Israel, including the establishment of kibbutzim and labor-oriented political parties.

**Implications for Modern Israeli Society and Policy**

The demographic changes resulting from European migration have had lasting implications for modern Israeli society and policy. The dominance of Ashkenazi (European-descended) Jews in the early years of the state led to the establishment of social and political institutions that reflected European values and norms. This dominance has shaped Israeli society in numerous ways, from the cultural emphasis on Western traditions to the policies that govern land use, settlement, and immigration.

One significant implication of the European migration is the ongoing tension between different Jewish communities in Israel. Ashkenazi Jews, who were the early pioneers of the Zionist movement and formed the majority of the leadership class, have historically held positions of power and influence. In contrast, Mizrahi and Sephardic Jews, who arrived later and often under more challenging circumstances, have faced discrimination and marginalization, both socially and economically. This has created a divide within Israeli society that persists to this day, with Ashkenazi Jews generally enjoying higher socioeconomic status compared to their non-European counterparts.

The demographic changes have also influenced Israeli policies, particularly with regard to land and settlement. The arrival of European Jews and the subsequent establishment of the state led to policies focused on expanding Jewish settlements and securing land for the growing Jewish population. These policies have often come at the expense of the Palestinian population, contributing to ongoing conflicts over land and resources. The settlement policies, which began in the early years of the state and continue to this day, have been a source of both domestic and international controversy, shaping Israel's relationships with its neighbors and with the broader global community.

Another significant policy implication is Israel's approach to immigration. The Law of Return, enacted in 1950, grants Jews from around the world the right to immigrate to Israel and obtain citizenship. This policy, which was designed to encourage Jewish migration and solidify a Jewish majority, reflects the influence of the early European Zionist ideals of creating a safe haven for Jews globally. While the policy has successfully increased the Jewish population, it has also led to debates about identity, inclusion, and the rights of non-Jewish residents, particularly the Palestinian population living in Israel and the occupied territories.

The impact of European migration on Israeli demographics has also influenced the country's foreign policy. The strong ties between Israel and Western nations, particularly the United States and various European countries, are rooted in part in the shared cultural and historical connections brought by European Jews. These relationships have provided Israel with significant diplomatic, financial, and military support, which has been crucial to its security and development. However, these ties have also influenced Israel's positioning in the broader Middle Eastern context, often aligning it with Western interests that may be at odds with those of its neighbors.

Overall, the impact of European migration on Israeli demographics has been profound, shaping the social, cultural, and political fabric of the nation. The demographic shifts brought about by European migration not only altered the balance of populations in the region but also established a foundation for the cultural and policy directions that Israel has taken in the decades since its founding. The legacy of this migration continues to influence the dynamics of Israeli society, contributing to both its diversity and its internal challenges as it navigates the complexities of its identity and relationships in the Middle East.

# Chapter 3: The Narrative of the 'Return' vs. Colonialism

Chapter 3 delves into the complex and often contradictory narratives surrounding the creation of Israel, examining the tension between the idea of a "return to the ancestral homeland" and the reality of colonialism. Central to Zionist ideology is the concept of a return—a belief that Jews are returning to a land that was historically and biblically theirs. This narrative has been deeply rooted in religious and historical justifications, with Zionist leaders invoking biblical references to frame the establishment of a Jewish state as both a fulfillment of divine promise and a historical right. The use of these religious and historical elements helped create a compelling story of rightful reclamation, resonating strongly with Jews around the world and gaining sympathy from international audiences.

However, the narrative of return has often been challenged by parallels to colonial settler strategies observed in other parts of the world. Many aspects of the Zionist movement and the establishment of Israel reflect characteristics typical of colonial ventures, particularly settler-colonialism, where settlers arrive with the intention of establishing a permanent presence, often at the expense of the indigenous population. By comparing Zionist settlement strategies with those of British colonies in Africa and India, this chapter highlights the similarities in methods of land acquisition, displacement of local populations, and the establishment of exclusive institutions that favored the settlers over the indigenous inhabitants.

Propaganda also played a crucial role in shaping the narrative of return, particularly in Europe and the Western world. Media campaigns, literature, and art were utilized to foster a sense of belonging and legitimacy, portraying the settlement of Palestine as a natural and just return of an exiled people. This narrative was powerful in creating international support for the Zionist cause and framing the establishment of Israel in a positive light. It allowed the movement to gain significant sympathy and backing from Western audiences who were often unaware of, or indifferent to, the consequences for the indigenous Palestinian population.

Counter-narratives from the indigenous populations offer a starkly different perspective on the events that led to the creation of Israel. Palestinian voices tell the story of dispossession and loss, where communities that had lived on the land for generations were displaced to make way for new settlers. Resistance movements that emerged in response to this dispossession provide important historical context, revealing the struggles faced by the Palestinian population as they confronted a project that, from their perspective, was not a rightful return but an act of colonization. By exploring these contrasting narratives, this chapter aims to provide a nuanced understanding of the creation of Israel and the divergent stories that continue to shape the conflict today.

# Zionist Ideology: Framing the 'Return to the Ancestral Homeland'

## THE RELIGIOUS AND HISTORICAL Justifications for "Return"

At the core of Zionist ideology lies the concept of the Jewish people's return to their ancestral homeland, a vision deeply embedded in both religious beliefs and historical narratives. The idea of return is rooted in the Jewish experience of exile, which dates back to ancient times when Jews were dispersed following the destruction of the First and Second Temples in Jerusalem. The concept of returning to the land of Israel has been a central theme in Jewish religious thought for centuries, reflected in prayers, rituals, and cultural expressions that emphasize the longing for Zion. This deep spiritual connection to the land has been a driving force behind the Zionist movement, providing a powerful justification for the establishment of a Jewish state in Palestine.

The religious argument for return is grounded in the belief that the land of Israel was divinely promised to the descendants of Abraham, Isaac, and Jacob. This promise, which appears in the Hebrew Bible, is seen as a covenant between God and the Jewish people, granting them the right to inhabit and govern the land. For many early Zionists, this religious narrative provided a sense of legitimacy and purpose, framing the movement as not only a political endeavor but also a fulfillment of divine will. The notion that Jews were returning to the land that had always belonged to them—despite the centuries of displacement—helped garner support among religious Jews who viewed the Zionist project as a sacred mission.

In addition to religious justifications, historical arguments have also been central to the Zionist narrative of return. The connection between the Jewish people and the land of Israel is well-documented in historical texts and archaeological evidence, which demonstrate the presence of Jewish communities in the region for thousands of years. By emphasizing this historical continuity, Zionist leaders sought to present their return to Palestine as the restoration of a legitimate and ancient claim, rather than a new colonial endeavor. This framing was particularly important in gaining international support, as it portrayed the Zionist movement as a people seeking to reclaim their lost homeland rather than as foreign settlers imposing themselves on an existing population.

**Use of Biblical References in Zionist Rhetoric**

The use of biblical references was a powerful tool in Zionist rhetoric, helping to solidify the idea of return in the minds of both Jews and non-Jews. The Hebrew Bible, with its numerous references to the land of Israel, provided a rich source of inspiration for Zionist leaders, who used these texts to evoke a sense of historical and spiritual connection to the land. Passages that spoke of the divine promise to Abraham, the exodus from Egypt, and the establishment of the Kingdom of Israel were frequently invoked to justify the claim to the land and to inspire Jewish communities around the world to support the cause.

Biblical references were also used to frame the hardships faced by early Zionist pioneers as part of a larger, divinely ordained mission. The struggles of early settlers—who faced difficult living conditions, conflicts with local populations, and the challenges of building a new society—were often compared to the biblical stories of the Israelites overcoming adversity in their journey to establish a homeland. This narrative helped to create a sense of purpose and resilience among the settlers, who saw themselves as part of a historical continuum that stretched back to the time of the patriarchs and prophets.

Zionist leaders also used biblical references strategically to appeal to Christian audiences, particularly in Europe and the United States. The idea of the Jewish return to the Holy Land resonated with many

Christians who viewed it as a fulfillment of biblical prophecy. By framing the Zionist movement in terms that aligned with Christian religious beliefs, Zionist leaders were able to gain support from influential Christian groups and political leaders, who saw the establishment of a Jewish state as a positive development in the unfolding of biblical history. This support was instrumental in securing international backing for the Zionist cause, particularly during the critical years leading up to the establishment of Israel in 1948.

The use of biblical rhetoric also played a role in shaping the Zionist narrative of the land itself. The portrayal of Palestine as the "Promised Land" helped to minimize the presence and rights of the indigenous Arab population, who were often depicted as outsiders or usurpers in a land that rightfully belonged to the Jews. By framing the return as the reclamation of a divinely promised inheritance, Zionist leaders sought to justify the displacement of Palestinians and the establishment of Jewish settlements. This narrative, which drew heavily on biblical imagery, helped to create a sense of inevitability around the Zionist project, portraying it as the fulfillment of an ancient and unbreakable covenant.

The religious and historical justifications for the return to the ancestral homeland, combined with the strategic use of biblical references, were central to the development and success of Zionist ideology. They provided a powerful framework that not only motivated Jewish communities to support the movement but also garnered international sympathy and legitimacy. By framing their project as a return rather than a colonization, Zionist leaders were able to create a compelling narrative that has had a lasting impact on the perception of Israel's origins and its right to exist as a Jewish state in the Middle East.

# Colonial Settler Strategies: Examining Parallels Between Israel and Other Colonies

**COMPARISON WITH BRITISH Colonies in Africa and India**

The establishment of Israel has been compared to other colonial ventures, particularly British colonies in Africa and India, where similar settler strategies and colonial practices were employed. In both contexts, European powers sought to control territories by implanting a settler population that could consolidate their claim to the land and create a new sociopolitical order. British colonies in Africa, such as Kenya and Rhodesia (now Zimbabwe), involved the settlement of Europeans who established their own governance structures and economic systems, often at the expense of the indigenous population. In India, British colonizers imposed political control and economic exploitation, benefiting a small group of colonists and their allies while marginalizing the native population.

In Palestine, the arrival of European Jews and the subsequent establishment of Israel involved strategies similar to those seen in British colonial projects. The land was portrayed as underutilized and in need of development, a common colonial trope used to justify settler occupation. Zionist leaders, much like the British colonial administrators in Africa and India, framed their presence as a civilizing mission, intending to bring progress, development, and modern governance to the region. This narrative was used to rationalize the appropriation of land and the displacement of the local population, in much the same way that European settlers in Africa and India justified their presence and control over indigenous lands.

The role of European powers, particularly Britain, also mirrors the colonial dynamics seen in Africa and India. During the British Mandate in Palestine, British authorities facilitated the settlement of European Jews, much as they had supported European settlement in other colonies. The use of legal and administrative tools to facilitate land acquisition and settlement expansion was a common colonial practice, employed to create a favorable environment for settlers while minimizing the rights of the native population. In this way, the Zionist project in Palestine was supported and legitimized by the same colonial structures that were used to establish and maintain British rule in other parts of the world.

**Settler-Colonialism: Key Characteristics and Practices**

The concept of settler-colonialism provides a framework for understanding the parallels between Israel and other colonial projects. Unlike traditional colonialism, which often involves the exploitation of a territory's resources for the benefit of a distant imperial power, settler-colonialism is characterized by the establishment of a permanent settler population that seeks to displace and replace the indigenous inhabitants. This type of colonialism is marked by a focus on land acquisition, the establishment of new social and political institutions, and the erasure or marginalization of the indigenous population.

One of the key characteristics of settler-colonialism is the emphasis on land as the central asset. In the case of Israel, the acquisition of land for Jewish settlement was a primary goal of the Zionist movement. Land purchases, often facilitated by foreign donors and supported by British mandate authorities, allowed the Jewish community to establish a territorial foothold in Palestine. This focus on land mirrored the strategies used by settler-colonial projects in places like North America, Australia, and Africa, where settlers sought to secure land for farming, development, and the creation of new communities, often at the expense of the native population.

Another defining feature of settler-colonialism is the establishment of institutions that serve the needs of the settler population while excluding or marginalizing the indigenous people. In Palestine, the creation of Jewish institutions, such as the Jewish Agency and the Haganah (a paramilitary organization), allowed the settlers to establish their own governance structures, defense forces, and economic systems.

These institutions were designed to support the growth and security of the Jewish community, often without regard for the impact on the local Arab population. This pattern of exclusion is a hallmark of settler-colonialism, where the settlers create a parallel society that benefits from the resources of the land while denying the same opportunities to the indigenous inhabitants.

Settler-colonialism is also characterized by the use of narratives and myths to legitimize the presence of the settlers and justify the displacement of the native population. In the case of Israel, the narrative of "a land without a people for a people without a land" was used to frame Palestine as an empty, undeveloped territory awaiting Jewish settlement. This myth served to minimize the presence of the Arab population and justify their displacement, much as similar narratives were used by European settlers in North America and Australia to depict indigenous peoples as obstacles to progress and civilization. By framing their settlement as a rightful return to an ancestral homeland, Zionist leaders were able to gain support for their project and present it as a legitimate endeavor rather than a colonial conquest.

The parallels between Israel and other settler-colonial projects reveal the broader dynamics at play in the establishment of the state. The strategies of land acquisition, institutional exclusion, and the use of legitimizing narratives are not unique to Israel but are part of a broader pattern of settler-colonialism that has been seen in many parts of the world. Understanding these parallels helps to shed light on the historical and ongoing conflicts in the region, as the legacy of settler-colonialism continues to shape the relationships between Israelis and Palestinians and the struggle over land, rights, and sovereignty.

# The Role of Propaganda in Shaping the 'Return' Narrative

**MEDIA CAMPAIGNS AND Cultural Influence in Europe and Beyond**

Propaganda played a crucial role in shaping the narrative of the Zionist "return" to the ancestral homeland, influencing both Jewish and non-Jewish audiences in Europe and beyond. Media campaigns were instrumental in generating support for the Zionist movement, using persuasive imagery and messaging to frame the Jewish migration to Palestine as a legitimate and historically justified return. These campaigns often highlighted the hardships faced by Jews in Europe, portraying Palestine as the solution to centuries of persecution and statelessness. By framing the return in these terms, Zionist propaganda appealed to a wide range of audiences, from Jewish communities seeking a safe haven to non-Jewish supporters who viewed the movement as a humanitarian cause.

In Europe and the United States, Zionist organizations used newspapers, pamphlets, posters, and other forms of mass media to shape public perception. The use of emotive imagery—depicting Jews as pioneers reclaiming a barren land—evoked sympathy and admiration, drawing on familiar colonial tropes of bringing civilization to untamed territories. These campaigns were designed to counter opposition to Jewish migration, emphasizing the agricultural development and modernization brought by Jewish settlers. The portrayal of Palestine as a land waiting to be redeemed resonated with both Jewish audiences, who felt a spiritual connection to the land, and Western audiences, who were influenced by colonial ideas of development and progress.

The influence of media extended beyond traditional propaganda channels. Zionist leaders were adept at leveraging public events, conferences, and political lobbying to spread their message and garner support from influential figures. The First Zionist Congress in 1897, for example, was not just a political event but also a highly publicized demonstration of Jewish unity and determination to establish a homeland. The outcomes of these gatherings were widely disseminated through media channels, further reinforcing the narrative of a people returning to their rightful land. This public relations effort helped to secure crucial diplomatic support from European powers, ultimately leading to the issuance of the Balfour Declaration and the British Mandate.

**The Role of Literature and Art in Creating a Narrative of Belonging**

Literature and art played a significant role in creating and sustaining the narrative of belonging to the land of Israel. Zionist writers and artists used their work to evoke a sense of historical continuity and emotional connection to the land, framing the return as both a physical and spiritual journey. Poetry, novels, and essays by prominent Zionist authors, such as Hayim Nahman Bialik and Theodor Herzl, were instrumental in cultivating a sense of shared identity among Jews worldwide. These works drew heavily on biblical imagery, linking the contemporary return to ancient events such as the Exodus from Egypt or the rebuilding of Jerusalem after the Babylonian exile. By invoking these powerful symbols, Zionist literature sought to inspire Jewish communities and instill a sense of purpose and destiny.

The portrayal of the land itself was a central theme in Zionist literature. Palestine was often depicted as a desolate, neglected land in need of redemption—a portrayal that conveniently overlooked the presence of the indigenous Arab population and their agricultural and cultural contributions. This image of a barren land awaiting its rightful caretakers served to justify the Zionist project, framing it as an act of restoration rather than colonization. The notion of "making the desert bloom" became a powerful metaphor for the Zionist endeavor, emphasizing the transformative power of Jewish settlement and reinforcing the idea that the land was intrinsically linked to the Jewish people.

Art also played a key role in shaping the narrative of return. Visual representations of the land, such as paintings, posters, and photographs, often depicted idealized landscapes of verdant fields, thriving orchards, and modern settlements, creating a vision of Palestine as a land of opportunity and prosperity. These images were used extensively in propaganda materials, emphasizing the success of Jewish pioneers in cultivating the land and building a new society. The imagery of strong, youthful pioneers working the land was designed to contrast with the stereotypical image of the downtrodden, urban Jew of Europe, presenting a new ideal of Jewish identity that was tied to the soil and the nation.

The cultural impact of these artistic and literary efforts was profound, helping to foster a sense of belonging and connection to the land among Jews who had never set foot in Palestine. This narrative of return became a central element of Zionist ideology, shaping the aspirations of generations of Jews and providing a powerful justification for the establishment of a Jewish state. It also played a role in shaping international perceptions of the Zionist project, garnering support from those who viewed the movement as a legitimate national revival rather than an act of colonialism.

Through media campaigns, literature, and art, the Zionist movement was able to construct a compelling narrative of return that resonated deeply with both Jewish and non-Jewish audiences. This narrative was not just about reclaiming land; it was about creating a sense of historical continuity, belonging, and destiny that legitimized the Zionist endeavor and laid the foundation for the creation of the state of Israel. The power of this propaganda in shaping both local and global perceptions of the Zionist project cannot be overstated, as it helped to secure the political, financial, and moral support necessary for the realization of a Jewish homeland.

# Counter-Narratives from Indigenous Populations and Historical Reality

**PALESTINIAN VOICES: The Dispossession Narrative**

The Zionist narrative of the "return to the ancestral homeland" has been met with strong counter-narratives from the indigenous Palestinian population, who experienced the events of the late 19th and 20th centuries very differently. From the Palestinian perspective, the establishment of Israel was not a rightful return but an act of dispossession and colonialism that led to the loss of their land, homes, and way of life. Palestinian voices emphasize that, contrary to the Zionist portrayal of Palestine as an empty land awaiting its rightful owners, the region was home to a vibrant and diverse population that had lived there for generations, cultivating the land and establishing communities.

The dispossession narrative is centered around the events of 1948, known to Palestinians as the Nakba, or "catastrophe." During the Nakba, an estimated 750,000 Palestinians were forcibly displaced from their homes, becoming refugees in neighboring countries or in other parts of Palestine. This mass displacement was accompanied by the destruction of hundreds of Palestinian villages, effectively erasing the physical presence of Palestinian communities from large areas of what would become the state of Israel. For Palestinians, these events represent a profound loss—both of their homeland and of their historical and cultural heritage. The Nakba has become a defining element of Palestinian identity, shaping their collective memory and informing their struggle for justice and recognition.

The dispossession narrative is also reinforced by the continued experience of displacement and marginalization. Palestinians in the occupied territories, as well as those who remained within the borders of Israel after 1948, have faced decades of land confiscation, restrictions on movement, and systemic discrimination. The expansion of Israeli settlements in the West Bank, the construction of the separation barrier, and the policies that limit Palestinian access to resources and economic opportunities are all seen as extensions of the original act of dispossession. These ongoing injustices are central to the Palestinian counter-narrative, which portrays the Zionist project as a form of settler-colonialism that seeks to replace the indigenous population with a new, predominantly European-descended community.

**Resistance Movements and Their Historical Context**

In response to the displacement and marginalization they experienced, Palestinians have engaged in various forms of resistance, which have become an integral part of their counter-narrative. The history of Palestinian resistance is marked by a series of uprisings, protests, and armed struggles aimed at opposing both British colonial rule during the Mandate period and, later, the establishment and expansion of the Israeli state. These resistance movements reflect the deep-rooted desire of Palestinians to reclaim their land and assert their rights, and they are often framed within the broader context of anti-colonial struggles around the world.

The first significant wave of Palestinian resistance occurred during the British Mandate, particularly in the 1920s and 1930s, when Palestinian Arabs organized protests and strikes against British policies that facilitated Jewish immigration and land acquisition. The Arab Revolt of 1936-1939 was a major uprising that sought to challenge both British authority and the growing influence of the Zionist movement. Although the revolt was ultimately suppressed, it highlighted the determination of the Palestinian population to resist the colonial policies that were leading to their displacement.

After the establishment of Israel in 1948, Palestinian resistance took on new forms, including the emergence of guerrilla groups and political organizations dedicated to the liberation of Palestine. The formation of the Palestine Liberation Organization (PLO) in 1964 marked a turning point in the Palestinian struggle, as it sought to unify various factions under a common goal of achieving self-determination and the right of return for refugees. The PLO's activities, including armed attacks against Israeli targets, were seen by many Palestinians as a legitimate response to the injustices they had endured, although these actions also drew international condemnation and were met with harsh reprisals by Israel.

The First Intifada (1987-1993) and the Second Intifada (2000-2005) were popular uprisings that involved mass protests, civil disobedience, and violent confrontations with Israeli forces. These uprisings were driven by widespread frustration with the ongoing occupation of Palestinian territories and the lack of progress toward a political solution. The First Intifada, in particular, brought international attention to the plight of Palestinians and led to increased pressure for a negotiated settlement. The Oslo Accords, which followed, were seen as a potential pathway to peace, but the failure to achieve a lasting resolution has left many Palestinians disillusioned, and the sense of dispossession remains a central grievance.

Palestinian resistance is not limited to armed struggle or mass uprisings; it also includes cultural and political efforts to assert their identity and tell their story. Palestinian writers, artists, and activists have played a crucial role in challenging the dominant Zionist narrative and presenting an alternative account of history—one that emphasizes the experiences of displacement, loss, and resilience. These cultural forms of resistance seek to preserve Palestinian heritage and ensure that the memory of the Nakba and the ongoing struggles of Palestinians are not forgotten.

The counter-narratives presented by the indigenous Palestinian population are essential for understanding the complexities of the Israeli-Palestinian conflict. They challenge the dominant narrative of a rightful return and highlight the colonial dimensions of the Zionist project, emphasizing the consequences for those who were displaced and marginalized. By examining these counter-narratives, it becomes clear that the conflict is not simply a matter of competing nationalisms but also a struggle over historical justice, recognition, and the right to self-determination.

# Chapter 4: Israel's Founding Myths and Reality

Chapter 4 focuses on the founding myths that have shaped the narrative of Israel's establishment and contrasts them with the historical realities of the region. One of the most pervasive myths is the idea that Palestine was "a land without a people for a people without a land," a phrase often used to justify the settlement of European Jews in the region. This narrative was instrumental in framing the Zionist project as one that was not displacing any significant population but rather reclaiming an empty or underutilized land. However, historical analysis reveals a very different reality—Palestine was home to a diverse and thriving population long before 1948, with established communities of Arabs, Christians, and Jews living in towns, cities, and rural areas. The portrayal of Palestine as an uninhabited or underdeveloped territory served as a colonial justification for the displacement of its indigenous inhabitants.

The demographic reality before and after the establishment of Israel further dispels the myth of an empty land. The events of 1948, known as the Nakba or "catastrophe" by Palestinians, led to the forced displacement of hundreds of thousands of Palestinian Arabs from their homes. This mass exodus dramatically altered the population of the region, setting in motion a series of demographic changes that continue to affect the political and social landscape today. The patterns of migration that followed the establishment of Israel, including the influx of Jewish immigrants and the creation of Palestinian refugee communities, reshaped the region and created long-lasting demographic tensions.

Colonial rhetoric played a key role in justifying the settlement of Palestine, drawing on narratives that have been used in colonial ventures around the world. The idea of a "civilizing mission," where settlers bring progress and development to a supposedly backward or empty land, was used to frame the Zionist movement in a positive light. This rhetoric not only served to legitimize land acquisition but also painted the indigenous population as obstacles to be overcome rather than as communities with their own legitimate claims and rights. Similar narratives have been employed in other colonial contexts, where the displacement of local populations was justified in the name of progress and civilization.

The impact of these founding myths continues to influence modern Israeli society. The narratives that were created during the establishment of Israel have been deeply embedded in political discourse and educational curricula, shaping the way Israelis perceive their history and their relationship with the land. These myths have become a foundation for national identity, affecting political decisions, social attitudes, and the ongoing conflict with the Palestinian population. By examining these myths and contrasting them with historical realities, this chapter aims to reveal the colonial underpinnings of Israel's founding narrative and the lasting impact these stories have had on both Israeli and Palestinian society.

# The Myth of "A Land Without a People": Historical Analysis

**THE ACTUAL DEMOGRAPHICS of Palestine Before 1948**

One of the most enduring myths associated with the Zionist movement is the idea that Palestine was "a land without a people for a people without a land." This phrase, often used to justify Jewish settlement in the region, suggested that Palestine was an empty or sparsely populated territory awaiting the arrival of the Jewish people. However, historical evidence clearly shows that Palestine was home to a well-established population long before the waves of Jewish migration in the late 19th and early 20th centuries. This population included a diverse mix of Muslim, Christian, and Jewish communities who had lived in the region for centuries, cultivating the land, building towns, and developing a vibrant culture.

Before 1948, Palestine had a predominantly Arab population, with significant numbers of Muslims and Christians living in cities such as Jerusalem, Jaffa, Haifa, and smaller rural communities. The Jewish population, while present, was much smaller, and it consisted primarily of communities that had lived in the region for centuries. Census records from the late Ottoman period and the British Mandate era provide a detailed picture of the demographic makeup of Palestine, indicating that the majority of the population was Arab, with a well-developed agricultural economy and thriving urban centers. Far from being an empty land, Palestine was a place with a rich cultural heritage and a diverse society.

The myth of an uninhabited or underpopulated land served to obscure the presence of this indigenous population and to frame the Zionist project as a benign effort to settle an empty, barren territory. This narrative conveniently ignored the reality of the existing Palestinian society, which had deep historical roots in the region. It also dismissed the contributions of Palestinian farmers, merchants, and artisans, who played a crucial role in the economic and social life of the country. By presenting Palestine as a land without a people, Zionist leaders sought to minimize the potential conflict with the existing population and to justify the acquisition of land for Jewish settlement.

**Colonial Justifications for Displacement**

The myth of "a land without a people" also served as a powerful colonial justification for the displacement of the indigenous Palestinian population. By framing Palestine as empty and undeveloped, Zionist leaders were able to portray their settlement efforts as a civilizing mission, similar to other colonial projects in Africa, the Americas, and Australia. This narrative aligned with broader colonial ideologies of the 19th and early 20th centuries, which depicted colonized territories as backward and in need of development, often to the exclusion of the native populations who had lived there for generations.

The language of improvement and development was frequently used by Zionist settlers to justify the appropriation of land. The slogan "making the desert bloom" became a central element of Zionist rhetoric, emphasizing the transformation of what was portrayed as neglected, barren land into productive agricultural settlements. This portrayal ignored the fact that much of the land being settled was already cultivated by Palestinian farmers, who had developed sophisticated agricultural practices suited to the local climate. The displacement of these farmers was often framed as a necessary part of bringing progress and modernization to the land, in line with the colonial logic that prioritized settler needs over the rights of the indigenous population.

The British Mandate authorities, who governed Palestine from 1920 to 1948, played a significant role in facilitating the Zionist project and its underlying colonial justifications. The British, driven by their own strategic interests in the Middle East, supported Jewish immigration and land acquisition through policies that favored the

Zionist cause. The legal and administrative framework established during the Mandate period allowed Jewish organizations to purchase land, often displacing Palestinian tenant farmers in the process. The resulting dispossession of Palestinian communities was justified through the lens of colonial development, with British and Zionist officials arguing that Jewish settlement would bring economic growth and modernization to the region.

The myth of an empty land also played a role in shaping international perceptions of the Zionist project. By presenting Palestine as a land without a people, Zionist leaders were able to garner sympathy and support from European and American audiences, who were often unaware of the actual demographics of the region. The portrayal of Jewish settlers as pioneers reclaiming an empty land resonated with Western audiences familiar with similar narratives from their own colonial histories, where settlers were seen as bringing civilization to untamed frontiers. This framing helped to legitimize the displacement of Palestinians and to obscure the realities of what was happening on the ground.

The historical analysis of the myth of "a land without a people" reveals the colonial underpinnings of the Zionist project and the ways in which this narrative was used to justify the displacement of the indigenous Palestinian population. By ignoring the presence and rights of the existing population, the myth provided a convenient rationale for settlement and land acquisition, framing the establishment of Israel as a natural and rightful return rather than an act of colonization. The legacy of this myth continues to shape the Israeli-Palestinian conflict today, as the dispossession of Palestinians and the denial of their historical presence remain central issues in the struggle for justice and recognition.

# Demographic Reality Before and After the Establishment of Israel

## THE 1948 NAKBA AND Its Demographic Impact

The establishment of Israel in 1948 marked a significant turning point in the demographic reality of Palestine, leading to dramatic shifts in the region's population. Known to Palestinians as the Nakba, or "catastrophe," the events of 1948 resulted in the mass displacement of hundreds of thousands of Palestinians from their homes. Approximately 750,000 Palestinians were forced to flee during the Arab-Israeli War, either driven out by direct military actions or fleeing out of fear as conflict spread across the region. This mass displacement resulted in the depopulation of entire villages and cities, fundamentally altering the demographic landscape of the area.

The Nakba had a profound impact on the Palestinian population, transforming a majority of them into refugees overnight. Many sought refuge in neighboring Arab countries, including Jordan, Lebanon, and Syria, while others found themselves internally displaced within what would become the West Bank and Gaza Strip. The sudden and large-scale displacement not only changed the physical demographics but also led to a profound psychological and cultural impact on the Palestinian people, who lost their homes, livelihoods, and connection to the land that had been theirs for generations.

In addition to the displacement, the Nakba led to the destruction of more than 500 Palestinian villages, which were either razed or repopulated with new Jewish immigrants. This destruction served both to remove the physical presence of Palestinian communities and to ensure that the refugees could not return to their homes. The demographic impact of the Nakba extended beyond the immediate loss of population; it also created a permanent refugee crisis, with millions of Palestinians and their descendants still living in refugee camps today, many of whom hold on to the hope and the right of return to their ancestral homes.

**Migration Patterns and Population Changes Post-1948**

Following the establishment of Israel, new migration patterns further reshaped the demographic landscape of the region. After 1948, Israel experienced significant Jewish immigration from various parts of the world, further solidifying the Jewish majority in the newly created state. Many of these immigrants were Holocaust survivors from Europe, driven by the desire to rebuild their lives after the horrors of World War II. Others came from Arab countries, where growing tensions and anti-Jewish sentiment prompted their departure. This influx of immigrants, often encouraged by the new Israeli government, aimed to increase the Jewish population and strengthen the fledgling state's position in the face of ongoing regional hostilities.

The arrival of Jewish immigrants from Europe and the Middle East after 1948 contributed to a rapid increase in Israel's population, which doubled within a few years. This immigration was facilitated by the Law of Return, enacted in 1950, which granted Jews around the world the right to immigrate to Israel and obtain citizenship. The state actively sought to encourage Jewish migration as a means of consolidating its demographic advantage, expanding its labor force, and ensuring its security. These efforts were largely successful, transforming Israel into a diverse society composed of Jews from Europe, the Middle East, North Africa, and, later, from the Soviet Union and Ethiopia.

The Palestinian population, meanwhile, faced ongoing displacement and demographic challenges. Those who remained within the borders of the newly established state of Israel were granted citizenship, but they faced systemic discrimination and restrictions on their movement, property rights, and access to resources. In contrast, the Palestinians who ended up in the West Bank and Gaza Strip found themselves under Jordanian and Egyptian control, respectively, until the Israeli occupation began in 1967. During this period, the refugee crisis remained unresolved, and the Palestinian population was largely excluded from political processes that determined their fate.

The Six-Day War of 1967 further altered the demographic situation in the region. Israel's occupation of the West Bank, Gaza Strip, and East Jerusalem brought millions of additional Palestinians under Israeli control, but without granting them the rights of citizenship. This created a complex demographic reality in which Israel held authority over a large Palestinian population while maintaining a Jewish majority within its recognized borders. The occupation also led to the establishment of Jewish settlements in the West Bank, further complicating the demographic and political landscape and contributing to the tensions that persist to this day.

Migration patterns after 1948 also included the continued displacement of Palestinians. Many Palestinian refugees who fled during the Nakba were unable to return due to Israeli policies that restricted their entry. Subsequent wars and conflicts, such as the 1967 war and the Lebanese Civil War, led to additional waves of displacement, further exacerbating the refugee crisis. The demographic impact of these conflicts has left millions of Palestinians living in diaspora communities throughout the Middle East and beyond, with many still holding refugee status and lacking permanent citizenship in their host countries.

The demographic changes before and after the establishment of Israel reflect the broader conflict over land, identity, and sovereignty. The Nakba and subsequent migration patterns have left a legacy of dispossession and displacement for the Palestinian population, while Jewish immigration has transformed Israel into a diverse, multiethnic society with a strong Jewish majority. These demographic realities continue to shape the political dynamics of the region, influencing the ongoing struggle for self-determination, recognition, and the right of return for Palestinian refugees. The interplay between these historical and ongoing population shifts lies at the heart of the Israeli-Palestinian conflict, highlighting the challenges of finding a just and lasting solution to the competing claims to the land.

# Colonial Rhetoric and Its Role in Justifying Settlement

**NARRATIVES OF 'CIVILIZING Missions' in Israel and Other Colonies**

The rhetoric of "civilizing missions" has long been a justification used by colonial powers to legitimize their actions, portraying their endeavors as efforts to bring progress and enlightenment to supposedly undeveloped or backward regions. This narrative was no different in the context of Zionist settlement in Palestine. The idea of making the "desert bloom" was a central theme in Zionist rhetoric, emphasizing that Jewish settlers were transforming barren and neglected land into fertile and productive agricultural communities. This portrayal was intended to frame the Zionist project as a noble endeavor, bringing modernization, development, and civilization to a land that had been overlooked and underutilized.

The use of civilizing mission rhetoric allowed Zionist leaders to present their actions as benevolent and justified, obscuring the displacement and marginalization of the indigenous Palestinian population. This narrative was similar to the rhetoric used by European colonial powers in Africa, Asia, and the Americas, who often portrayed their colonization efforts as necessary to uplift native populations. British colonial authorities, for example, justified their presence in India and Africa by claiming that they were bringing infrastructure, governance, and modern education to "primitive" societies, while disregarding the disruption and exploitation that came with colonial rule.

In Palestine, the civilizing mission narrative served to minimize the presence and contributions of the existing Arab population. The image of Palestine as a neglected land awaiting redemption suggested that the Palestinians who had lived there for generations were incapable of properly utilizing or caring for the land. This depiction effectively erased the rich agricultural practices, cultural heritage, and social structures that had existed in Palestine for centuries, replacing them with an image of empty or undeveloped territory in need of Jewish settlers to bring it to its full potential. By framing their settlement efforts in this way, Zionist leaders were able to present their project as beneficial not only to Jews but also to the broader world, portraying themselves as pioneers of progress and civilization.

**The Use of Myth to Legitimize Land Acquisition**

The use of myth has been a powerful tool in legitimizing land acquisition in colonial contexts, and the Zionist movement was no exception. One of the most pervasive myths used to justify the establishment of Jewish settlements in Palestine was the notion of "a land without a people for a people without a land." This myth suggested that Palestine was empty, underutilized, or lacked a cohesive population, thus making it available for settlement by Jews who were in need of a homeland. This narrative was crucial in garnering international support for the Zionist cause, as it presented the movement as a rightful return rather than an act of colonization.

The myth of an uninhabited land conveniently ignored the reality of the Palestinian population that had lived there for centuries, cultivating the land and establishing thriving communities. By perpetuating the idea that the land was essentially vacant, Zionist leaders were able to minimize the ethical concerns associated with displacing the indigenous population. This narrative also helped to justify the acquisition of land through legal and administrative means, often facilitated by the British authorities during the Mandate period. Land purchases by Jewish organizations were framed as legitimate transactions, even when they resulted in the displacement of Palestinian tenant farmers who had lived on and worked the land for generations.

The myth of an empty land was not unique to the Zionist movement; it was a common trope used by colonial powers throughout history to justify the appropriation of land. In North America, European settlers described the continent as a vast, empty wilderness, disregarding the presence of Indigenous peoples who had complex societies and established territories. In Australia, British colonizers used the concept of "terra nullius" (land belonging to no one) to legitimize their claims, ignoring the Aboriginal populations who had lived there for tens of thousands of years. These myths served to erase the presence of indigenous populations and to frame colonial settlement as a moral and legal endeavor.

In addition to the myth of an empty land, Zionist rhetoric also drew on biblical narratives to legitimize land acquisition. The idea of returning to the "Promised Land" was a powerful motivator for Jewish settlers and provided a sense of divine legitimacy to the Zionist project. By framing their actions as a fulfillment of a biblical promise, Zionist leaders were able to present their settlement efforts as part of a larger historical and spiritual mission, rather than as a political or colonial enterprise. This use of religious myth helped to rally support among Jews worldwide and to gain sympathy from Christian audiences who viewed the return of the Jewish people to Israel as a fulfillment of prophecy.

The reliance on colonial rhetoric and myth to justify settlement had significant implications for the indigenous Palestinian population. It not only provided a rationale for their displacement but also shaped the way they were perceived by the international community. By portraying Palestine as an empty or underdeveloped land, Zionist leaders were able to shift attention away from the consequences of settlement for the existing population. This framing contributed to the marginalization of Palestinian voices and the denial of their rights, as their presence and claims to the land were effectively rendered invisible by the dominant narrative.

Understanding the role of colonial rhetoric and myth in justifying the settlement of Palestine helps to shed light on the broader dynamics of the Israeli-Palestinian conflict. These narratives were instrumental in shaping international perceptions of the Zionist project and in providing the ideological foundation for the establishment of Israel. However, they also laid the groundwork for the displacement and dispossession of the Palestinian people, creating a legacy of conflict and inequality that persists to this day.

# The Impact of Founding Myths on Modern Israeli Society

## HOW FOUNDING MYTHS Affect Modern Politics

The founding myths of Israel, such as the idea of "a land without a people for a people without a land" and the narrative of a rightful return to an ancestral homeland, have had a profound impact on modern Israeli politics. These myths have shaped national identity, political discourse, and policy decisions, creating a framework in which the legitimacy of the state and its actions are tied to historical and religious narratives. The portrayal of Israel as the fulfillment of a divine promise or as the culmination of a historical return has been instrumental in justifying policies related to settlement, land acquisition, and security.

The myth of return plays a crucial role in shaping Israeli politics, particularly in relation to the ongoing conflict with the Palestinians. This narrative has been used to legitimize the expansion of Jewish settlements in the West Bank and East Jerusalem, areas that are viewed by many Israelis as part of the biblical homeland. Political leaders often draw on these founding myths to garner public support for settlement policies, portraying the expansion as a continuation of the historical mission of reclaiming and developing the land. This has led to the entrenchment of settlement activities, despite international opposition and the negative impact on the prospects for peace with the Palestinians.

The influence of founding myths is also evident in the way Israeli politics approaches issues of security and territorial control. The narrative of a people returning to their rightful land after centuries of persecution has fostered a sense of vulnerability and the need for self-defense, which has been central to the formation of Israeli security policy. The emphasis on security and the perceived existential threats to the state are often linked to the historical experiences of Jews in exile, reinforcing the idea that the state must be vigilant in protecting itself from external and internal threats. This has contributed to a political climate in which military solutions are often prioritized over diplomatic engagement, particularly in dealings with the Palestinian population.

## Educational Curricula and the Perpetuation of Colonial Narratives

The founding myths of Israel are also perpetuated through the educational system, where they play a key role in shaping the way history is taught and understood by new generations. The Israeli educational curricula often emphasize the historical and biblical connection between the Jewish people and the land of Israel, portraying the establishment of the state as a fulfillment of a long-awaited return. This narrative is woven into textbooks, history lessons, and national commemorations, creating a shared understanding of the state's origins that aligns with the founding myths.

The portrayal of the Zionist movement in educational materials often highlights the pioneering spirit of the early settlers and their efforts to "make the desert bloom," while downplaying or omitting the presence and experiences of the indigenous Palestinian population. The myth of an empty or neglected land awaiting redemption is reinforced, framing Jewish settlement as a positive and necessary development. This selective presentation of history serves to legitimize the actions taken during the establishment of the state and to create a sense of pride and entitlement among students regarding their connection to the land.

The absence of Palestinian perspectives from the curriculum further reinforces the founding myths and their colonial undertones. The experiences of Palestinian displacement, the destruction of villages during the Nakba, and the ongoing challenges faced by Palestinians in the occupied territories are often minimized or ignored altogether. By excluding these narratives, the educational system perpetuates a one-sided view of history that fails to acknowledge the complexities of the conflict and the impact of Zionist settlement on the indigenous population. This has contributed to a lack of understanding and empathy among many Israelis regarding the Palestinian perspective, making it more difficult to foster dialogue and reconciliation.

The perpetuation of founding myths through education also influences attitudes toward political solutions to the conflict. By framing the establishment of Israel as a rightful return and presenting the land as inherently belonging to the Jewish people, the educational system contributes to a sense of legitimacy regarding policies that prioritize Jewish settlement and control over the entire territory. This has implications for public support for initiatives such as the two-state solution, as many Israelis have been taught to view the entirety of the land as part of their historical and cultural heritage, making concessions more difficult to accept.

The impact of founding myths on modern Israeli society is thus multifaceted, affecting both political decision-making and the way history is understood and internalized by citizens. These myths have provided a powerful narrative that legitimizes the state's actions and reinforces national identity, but they have also contributed to the marginalization of Palestinian voices and the perpetuation of colonial attitudes. By examining the role of these myths in shaping politics and education, it becomes clear that they continue to play a significant role in defining the parameters of the Israeli-Palestinian conflict and the prospects for a just and lasting resolution.

# Chapter 5: Marginalization of Indigenous Populations

Chapter 5 explores the marginalization of indigenous populations in the context of Israel's establishment and subsequent policies, focusing on both Palestinian communities and non-European Jewish groups. The displacement of native Palestinians is a key aspect of the story, beginning with the events of 1948, often referred to as the Nakba, during which hundreds of thousands of Palestinians were forcibly displaced from their homes. This process of displacement continued in subsequent wars and conflicts, leading to a protracted refugee crisis that affected not only Palestinians but also neighboring countries that struggled to accommodate the influx of refugees. These displacements have had far-reaching consequences, creating generations of Palestinians living in exile, often in difficult and uncertain conditions.

The impact of Israeli policies on Palestinian communities has been profound, especially in terms of land confiscation and settlement expansion. The confiscation of land, often to make way for Jewish settlements, has significantly reduced the territory available to Palestinians and has fragmented their communities. This process, which continues to this day, has led to the establishment of a complex network of settlements, roads, and barriers that further isolate Palestinian communities from one another. The legal status of Palestinians living in the occupied territories is another significant factor contributing to their marginalization. Palestinians in these areas face a range of restrictions on their movement, property rights, and access to essential services, highlighting the unequal treatment they receive compared to Israeli settlers.

The marginalization within Israeli society extends beyond the Palestinian population to include non-European Jews, such as Mizrahi and Ethiopian Jews. Despite their contributions to the state of Israel, these communities have faced significant discrimination and exclusion. Mizrahi Jews, who came from Middle Eastern and North African countries, have often been treated as second-class citizens compared to their European Ashkenazi counterparts. Ethiopian Jews, who immigrated to Israel in more recent decades, have also faced systemic discrimination and challenges in integrating into Israeli society, including disparities in education, employment, and housing. This cultural and socioeconomic inequality underscores the hierarchical nature of Israeli society, which has historically favored Jews of European descent.

The chapter also examines the use of colonial tactics, specifically the "divide and rule" strategy, in the context of Israel's treatment of both Palestinians and Jewish communities. The fragmentation of Palestinian territories through settlement expansion, barriers, and administrative divisions mirrors colonial practices aimed at weakening resistance by dividing the population. Additionally, the differential treatment of Jewish communities based on their origins reflects a colonial mindset, where certain groups are privileged over others to maintain control and prevent unity. By exploring these dynamics, the chapter highlights the ongoing impact of colonial practices on the marginalized populations within and around Israel, shedding light on the systemic inequalities that continue to shape the region today.

# The Displacement of Native Palestinians: A Historical Overview

**FORCED DISPLACEMENTS: 1948 and Subsequent Wars**

The displacement of native Palestinians began in earnest during the events of 1948, a period known by Palestinians as the Nakba, or "catastrophe." The establishment of the state of Israel and the ensuing Arab-Israeli War resulted in the forced displacement of approximately 750,000 Palestinians from their homes. Many Palestinians were expelled by advancing Jewish militias, while others fled out of fear as violence spread throughout the region. Entire villages were depopulated, and many of these were subsequently destroyed or repopulated by Jewish settlers, effectively erasing the physical and cultural presence of the Palestinian communities that once inhabited these areas.

The displacements of 1948 were not isolated incidents but were part of a broader strategy to secure territory for the newly established state and ensure a Jewish demographic majority. As Jewish forces gained control of towns and villages, Palestinians were often forcibly removed, and their properties were confiscated. The exodus of Palestinians from urban centers such as Haifa, Jaffa, and Lydda, as well as from hundreds of rural villages, fundamentally altered the demographic makeup of the region, transforming large areas of what had been a predominantly Arab territory into a Jewish-majority state.

The displacement did not end with the Nakba. Subsequent wars and conflicts continued to displace Palestinians and prevent those who had fled in 1948 from returning. The 1967 Six-Day War, during which Israel occupied the West Bank, Gaza Strip, and East Jerusalem, resulted in another wave of displacement, with hundreds of thousands of Palestinians being uprooted once again. Many who had initially been displaced in 1948 found themselves becoming refugees for a second time. The Israeli occupation of these territories also led to policies that further marginalized Palestinians, including land confiscations, settlement expansion, and restrictions on movement, all of which contributed to ongoing displacement and the fragmentation of Palestinian communities.

**The Refugee Crisis and Its Impact on Neighboring Countries**

The displacement of Palestinians in 1948 and subsequent conflicts created a protracted refugee crisis that continues to have profound effects on the region. Many of the Palestinians who were expelled or fled during the Nakba sought refuge in neighboring countries, including Jordan, Lebanon, Syria, and Egypt. These refugees were often housed in makeshift camps, with the expectation that their displacement would be temporary and that they would soon be able to return to their homes. However, as the years passed, it became clear that a return was unlikely, and these camps evolved into more permanent settlements, with multiple generations of Palestinians growing up as refugees.

Jordan absorbed the largest number of Palestinian refugees, and many of them were eventually granted Jordanian citizenship, allowing them to integrate more fully into Jordanian society. However, even with citizenship, Palestinian refugees in Jordan have often faced challenges related to economic opportunities and social integration. In Lebanon and Syria, the situation has been more precarious. Palestinian refugees in these countries have generally not been granted citizenship and face significant restrictions on employment, property ownership, and access to social services. The lack of legal status has left many Palestinian refugees in Lebanon and Syria in a state of limbo, with limited rights and few prospects for the future.

The refugee crisis has also had a significant impact on the political dynamics of the region. The presence of large Palestinian refugee populations in neighboring countries has been a source of tension, both within these countries and between them and Israel. In Lebanon, the influx of Palestinian refugees contributed to the sectarian tensions that eventually led to the Lebanese Civil War, while in Jordan, the presence of Palestinian militant groups led to conflict with the Jordanian government in the early 1970s, culminating in the events known as "Black September." The ongoing plight of Palestinian refugees has also been a central issue in the broader Arab-Israeli conflict, with the right of return remaining a key demand of the Palestinian leadership and a major point of contention in peace negotiations.

The displacement of native Palestinians and the resulting refugee crisis are central to understanding the Israeli-Palestinian conflict and its enduring nature. The loss of homes, land, and livelihoods has had a lasting impact on Palestinian society, creating a sense of dispossession and injustice that continues to fuel resistance to Israeli occupation and demands for a just resolution. The refugees' demand for the right of return, enshrined in United Nations Resolution 194, remains a cornerstone of the Palestinian national movement, symbolizing their ongoing connection to the land from which they were displaced and their refusal to accept the permanence of their exile.

The historical overview of the displacement of Palestinians highlights the human cost of the conflict and the enduring legacy of the events of 1948 and subsequent wars. The forced displacements and the creation of a protracted refugee crisis have shaped the experiences and identities of millions of Palestinians, both those living in the occupied territories and those in diaspora communities across the Middle East and beyond. Addressing this legacy is essential for any meaningful resolution to the conflict, as the rights and aspirations of Palestinian refugees remain at the heart of the struggle for justice and peace in the region.

# The Impact of Israeli Policies on Palestinian Communities

**LAND CONFISCATION AND Settlement Expansion**

Israeli policies of land confiscation and settlement expansion have had a profound impact on Palestinian communities, fundamentally altering the physical, social, and economic landscape of the West Bank and East Jerusalem. Since the 1967 Six-Day War, Israel has occupied these territories, and one of the most significant aspects of its control has been the systematic expropriation of Palestinian land for the construction of Israeli settlements. These settlements, which are considered illegal under international law, have expanded over the decades, creating a fragmented and segregated landscape in which Palestinian communities are increasingly isolated and deprived of essential resources.

Land confiscation has been carried out under a variety of legal pretexts, including the declaration of areas as "state land," the appropriation of land for military purposes, or the designation of areas as nature reserves. These legal maneuvers have allowed Israel to seize large tracts of Palestinian land, often displacing families who have lived there for generations. The construction of the separation barrier, which Israel began building in 2002, has also led to the confiscation of significant amounts of Palestinian land. The barrier, which runs deep into the West Bank in many areas, has effectively annexed fertile agricultural land and water resources, cutting off Palestinian farmers from their livelihoods.

Settlement expansion has further compounded the impact of land confiscation on Palestinian communities. Israeli settlements are typically built on confiscated Palestinian land and are connected by a network of bypass roads that are restricted for use by settlers, further restricting Palestinian movement. The growth of settlements has created a fragmented geography in which Palestinian towns and villages are separated by settlement blocs, military zones, and roads, making travel between Palestinian areas difficult and time-consuming. This fragmentation has not only affected the social cohesion of Palestinian communities but has also hindered access to education, healthcare, and economic opportunities.

The expansion of settlements has also contributed to the displacement of Palestinian residents. Settlers, often supported by the Israeli government and military, have taken over Palestinian homes and land, sometimes through acts of violence or intimidation. The presence of settlers has led to frequent clashes, with Palestinian communities bearing the brunt of both settler violence and military interventions. The result has been a climate of fear and uncertainty, with many Palestinians forced to abandon their homes or lands due to the ongoing harassment and lack of protection from Israeli authorities.

### The Legal Status of Palestinians in Occupied Territories

The legal status of Palestinians in the occupied territories is another critical factor that has shaped their lives under Israeli rule. Palestinians in the West Bank, East Jerusalem, and Gaza Strip live under a complex and fragmented legal regime that has created a system of inequality and discrimination. In the West Bank, Palestinians are subject to Israeli military law, while Israeli settlers living in the same territory are governed by Israeli civil law, creating a dual legal system in which Palestinians have significantly fewer rights and protections.

The military legal system to which Palestinians are subject includes restrictions on movement, arbitrary detention, and the lack of due process. Palestinians in the West Bank must obtain permits from Israeli authorities for a wide range of activities, including traveling between different areas, building or renovating homes, and even accessing certain agricultural lands. The permit system, combined with the presence of numerous checkpoints and roadblocks, severely restricts the movement of Palestinians, impacting their ability to access healthcare, education, and employment. The military courts that handle cases involving Palestinians have been widely criticized for their lack of fairness, with high conviction rates and limited rights for defendants.

In East Jerusalem, the situation is different but still marked by significant discrimination. Following the 1967 war, Israel unilaterally annexed East Jerusalem, a move not recognized by the international community. Palestinians living in East Jerusalem were granted the status of "permanent residents" rather than citizens, meaning they do not have the same rights as Israeli citizens and can lose their residency status if they are unable to prove that Jerusalem is their "center of life." This precarious status leaves many Palestinians in East Jerusalem vulnerable to displacement, as they face bureaucratic hurdles in obtaining permits for housing, and their homes are often at risk of demolition if they are deemed to have been built without the required permissions—permissions that are notoriously difficult for Palestinians to obtain.

In Gaza, the situation is even more dire. Following Israel's disengagement from Gaza in 2005, the territory has been subject to a blockade that severely restricts the movement of people and goods. While Israel no longer has a permanent military presence inside Gaza, it maintains control over the airspace, territorial waters, and most border crossings, effectively isolating the territory from the outside world. The blockade, combined with frequent military operations, has had a devastating impact on the economy and infrastructure of Gaza, leading to widespread poverty, unemployment, and a humanitarian crisis.

The unequal legal status of Palestinians in the occupied territories has created a system of systemic discrimination that affects every aspect of their lives. The dual legal system, the restrictions on movement, and the precarious status of residency are all part of a broader policy framework designed to maintain control over the Palestinian population while facilitating the expansion of Israeli settlements. These policies have led to a situation in which Palestinians are effectively treated as second-class residents in their own land, with limited rights and opportunities compared to the Israeli settlers who live alongside them.

The impact of Israeli policies on Palestinian communities, through land confiscation, settlement expansion, and the imposition of discriminatory legal regimes, has created a deeply unequal reality in which Palestinians face ongoing displacement, restricted freedoms, and a lack of basic rights. Addressing these inequalities is essential for any meaningful resolution to the conflict, as the current policies have not only entrenched the occupation but have also perpetuated a cycle of dispossession and marginalization that fuels resentment and undermines the prospects for peace.

# Marginalization of Middle Eastern and African Jews in Israeli Society

## TREATMENT OF MIZRAHI and Ethiopian Jews

The integration of Jews from Middle Eastern and African countries, known as Mizrahi and Ethiopian Jews, into Israeli society has been marked by significant challenges and systemic discrimination. Mizrahi Jews, who came to Israel from countries such as Iraq, Yemen, Morocco, and Iran, and Ethiopian Jews, who arrived in large numbers during the 1980s and 1990s, have often been treated as second-class citizens compared to their Ashkenazi (European-descended) counterparts. The treatment of these communities has been characterized by cultural prejudice, economic marginalization, and a lack of equal opportunities.

When Mizrahi Jews began migrating to Israel in large numbers during the 1950s and 1960s, they faced a society that was dominated by Ashkenazi culture and norms. The early Zionist leadership, largely composed of European Jews, viewed Mizrahi Jews as culturally backward and in need of modernization. Many Mizrahi immigrants were settled in transit camps, often in remote areas or in towns that lacked infrastructure and economic opportunities. They faced significant barriers to integration, including poor housing conditions, limited access to quality education, and exclusion from the political and economic centers of power. These early experiences of discrimination laid the groundwork for the socioeconomic disparities that continue to affect Mizrahi Jews today.

Ethiopian Jews faced similar, and in some cases more severe, challenges when they began arriving in Israel. The Ethiopian Jewish community, known as Beta Israel, faced skepticism and discrimination from the broader Israeli society, which questioned their Jewishness and often treated them as outsiders. Many Ethiopian immigrants were placed in absorption centers where they were subjected to lengthy processes to "prove" their Jewishness before being allowed to integrate into mainstream society. The transition was particularly difficult for Ethiopian Jews, who had to adapt to an entirely different culture and faced systemic barriers in accessing education, housing, and employment. The discrimination they faced was often overt, including cases where Ethiopian blood donations were discarded due to unfounded fears of disease transmission, highlighting the prejudice that existed within the system.

**Cultural Discrimination and Socioeconomic Inequality**

The marginalization of Mizrahi and Ethiopian Jews has also been evident in the cultural domain, where Ashkenazi norms and traditions have dominated Israeli society. The early Zionist narrative emphasized the return of European Jews to their ancestral homeland, and as a result, Ashkenazi culture became the default for the emerging Israeli identity. This cultural dominance marginalized the traditions, languages, and customs of Mizrahi and Ethiopian Jews, who were often pressured to assimilate and abandon their heritage in favor of the more "modern" Ashkenazi culture. The erasure of their cultural identity contributed to a sense of alienation and exclusion, as their contributions to Israeli society were often undervalued or ignored.

Cultural discrimination against Mizrahi and Ethiopian Jews has also been perpetuated through the education system and the media. For many years, Israeli schools taught a version of history that largely focused on the experiences of European Jews, minimizing the rich cultural heritage of Jews from the Middle East and Africa. Textbooks and curricula often portrayed Mizrahi Jews as latecomers to the Zionist project, failing to recognize their deep historical connection to the land of Israel and their contributions to Jewish culture. In the media, Mizrahi and Ethiopian Jews were frequently depicted in stereotypical and negative ways, reinforcing prejudices and contributing to their social marginalization.

The cultural discrimination faced by Mizrahi and Ethiopian Jews has had significant socioeconomic implications. Mizrahi Jews continue to be underrepresented in higher education, high-paying jobs, and positions of political power. Many live in poorer neighborhoods and have limited access to quality public services, perpetuating cycles of poverty and disadvantage. Ethiopian Jews face even greater challenges, with high rates of unemployment, poverty, and school dropout compared to the rest of the population. The barriers to economic advancement have been compounded by discriminatory practices in the labor market, where Mizrahi and Ethiopian Jews are often paid less than their Ashkenazi counterparts for the same work or are excluded from certain professions altogether.

The inequality experienced by these communities is also reflected in the political landscape of Israel. Although Mizrahi Jews make up a significant portion of the population, they have historically been underrepresented in the Israeli government and key institutions. The dominance of Ashkenazi elites in political parties and government bodies has limited the ability of Mizrahi and Ethiopian Jews to influence policies that directly affect their lives. While there have been efforts in recent years to increase representation, these communities still face significant barriers to achieving equal political power.

Despite these challenges, there have been important efforts by Mizrahi and Ethiopian Jews to assert their rights and demand equality within Israeli society. Social movements led by Mizrahi activists have sought to challenge the cultural and economic marginalization of their community, calling for greater recognition of their heritage and equal opportunities. Ethiopian Jews have also organized protests against police brutality, discrimination, and unequal treatment, drawing attention to the systemic racism that they face. These movements have helped to raise awareness of the issues affecting these communities and have pushed for changes in government policy and public attitudes.

The marginalization of Middle Eastern and African Jews in Israeli society is a complex issue rooted in the historical dominance of Ashkenazi culture and the discriminatory practices that have shaped Israeli society since its founding. The treatment of Mizrahi and Ethiopian Jews reflects broader patterns of cultural discrimination and socioeconomic inequality, which continue to affect their lives in significant ways. Addressing these disparities requires not only policy changes to promote equal opportunities but also a shift in the cultural narrative to recognize and value the diverse contributions of all Jewish communities to Israeli society.

# European Colonial Tactics: Divide and Rule in Practice

## FRAGMENTATION OF PALESTINIAN Territories

The fragmentation of Palestinian territories is a tactic that echoes the "divide and rule" strategies commonly used by European colonial powers to maintain control over colonized populations. By breaking up territories and creating divisions among local communities, colonial authorities sought to prevent unified resistance and maintain dominance. In the Israeli-Palestinian context, the fragmentation of Palestinian territories has been achieved through a combination of settlement expansion, the construction of physical barriers, and administrative divisions that have made it difficult for Palestinians to establish a cohesive political or social entity.

Since the 1967 Six-Day War, Israel has occupied the West Bank, Gaza Strip, and East Jerusalem, and over time, it has implemented policies that have effectively divided these areas into isolated enclaves. In the West Bank, Israeli settlements, military zones, and bypass roads have fragmented Palestinian towns and villages, separating communities from each other and restricting movement. The construction of the separation barrier, which cuts deep into the West Bank in many places, has further divided Palestinian communities, leaving some towns and villages completely surrounded by the barrier and cut off from neighboring areas. This fragmentation has severely impacted the ability of Palestinians to travel, access education, healthcare, and employment, and maintain social connections.

In Gaza, the situation is even more extreme. Following Israel's disengagement from Gaza in 2005, the territory has been subjected to a blockade that has effectively isolated it from the outside world. The blockade, along with repeated military operations, has left Gaza in a state of economic and humanitarian crisis, with limited access to resources and opportunities for development. The separation of Gaza from the West Bank has made it difficult for Palestinians to maintain unity, both politically and socially, further weakening their ability to resist occupation and advocate for their rights.

The fragmentation of Palestinian territories serves to undermine the possibility of a viable Palestinian state, as it prevents the establishment of contiguous and autonomous areas that could form the basis for self-governance. By creating a situation in which Palestinian communities are divided and isolated from each other, Israeli policies have made it difficult for Palestinians to organize politically, maintain economic stability, and develop the infrastructure necessary for statehood. This tactic of dividing the population to weaken resistance is a classic colonial strategy, employed to maintain control and prevent the emergence of a strong, unified opposition.

**Differential Treatment of Jewish Communities Based on Origin**

The divide and rule tactic is not only applied to Palestinian communities but also extends to the treatment of different Jewish communities within Israeli society. Since the establishment of the state, Israeli society has been marked by significant divisions based on the origins of Jewish immigrants. The early Zionist leadership, which was predominantly composed of European (Ashkenazi) Jews, established a hierarchy in which Jews of Middle Eastern and North African origin (Mizrahi Jews) and, later, Ethiopian Jews were treated as second-class citizens. This differential treatment has created divisions within the Jewish population, undermining the potential for solidarity and cohesion.

Mizrahi Jews, who came to Israel from countries such as Iraq, Yemen, and Morocco, faced significant discrimination upon their arrival. They were often settled in underdeveloped areas, placed in transit camps, and given limited opportunities for social and economic advancement. The Ashkenazi-dominated leadership viewed Mizrahi

Jews as culturally inferior and in need of modernization, leading to policies that marginalized their traditions and excluded them from positions of power and influence. This created a clear division within Israeli society, with Ashkenazi Jews occupying the upper echelons of politics, business, and culture, while Mizrahi Jews were relegated to the margins.

The arrival of Ethiopian Jews in the 1980s and 1990s added another layer to this division. Ethiopian Jews, who came to Israel under highly challenging circumstances, faced systemic discrimination and skepticism regarding their Jewishness. They were often placed in absorption centers, where they were isolated from mainstream society and subjected to processes that questioned their identity and traditions. This treatment further reinforced the hierarchy within Israeli society, with Ethiopian Jews facing even greater barriers to integration and equal opportunity compared to Mizrahi Jews.

The differential treatment of Jewish communities based on their origin has created lasting divisions within Israeli society, contributing to socioeconomic inequality and cultural discrimination. The Ashkenazi elite has historically maintained control over political institutions, economic resources, and cultural narratives, limiting the opportunities for Mizrahi and Ethiopian Jews to achieve equal status. This divide and rule tactic serves to maintain the dominance of the Ashkenazi leadership, while preventing the emergence of a unified Jewish community that could challenge the existing power structures.

The impact of these divisions is evident in the socioeconomic disparities that persist within Israeli society. Mizrahi and Ethiopian Jews are more likely to live in poorer neighborhoods, have lower levels of education, and face discrimination in the labor market. These inequalities have led to frustration and resentment, resulting in social tensions and protests against the systemic discrimination that these communities face. The divide and rule strategy employed by the early Zionist leadership has thus had a lasting impact on the structure of

Israeli society, creating divisions that continue to affect the lives of many Israelis today.

By employing colonial tactics of divide and rule, both in the fragmentation of Palestinian territories and in the differential treatment of Jewish communities, Israeli policies have succeeded in maintaining control over the population while preventing the emergence of unified resistance. These strategies have contributed to the deep inequalities and divisions that characterize both Israeli and Palestinian societies, making the prospects for peace and reconciliation even more challenging. Understanding these tactics is essential for recognizing the obstacles to achieving a just and lasting resolution to the conflict, as they reveal the underlying dynamics of power and control that continue to shape the region.

# Chapter 6: Integration Challenges of Non-European Jewish Communities

Chapter 6 delves into the integration challenges faced by non-European Jewish communities in Israel, particularly Mizrahi and Sephardic Jews. These communities, whose roots lie in the Middle East and North Africa, have a distinct cultural identity and history that sets them apart from the European Ashkenazi Jews who largely shaped the founding of Israel. The migration of Mizrahi and Sephardic Jews to Israel, particularly in the years following the state's establishment, was marked by significant struggles, as these immigrants faced cultural dislocation and systemic discrimination. Despite their rich cultural heritage and contributions to Israeli society, they were often viewed through a lens of prejudice and treated as inferior compared to their Ashkenazi counterparts.

The discrimination experienced by Mizrahi and Sephardic Jews manifests in various socioeconomic disparities that persist to this day. Employment opportunities, income levels, and access to quality education have all been areas where these communities have faced systemic barriers, leading to significant disparities compared to the Ashkenazi population. This chapter examines how these disparities extend into the political sphere, where Mizrahi and Sephardic Jews have historically been underrepresented in positions of power and influence. Their limited representation in government institutions has further marginalized their voices and hindered efforts to address their unique challenges.

The dominance of European-Ashkenazi culture in Israel has contributed to the ongoing marginalization of non-European Jewish communities. Ashkenazi cultural hegemony is evident in the prominence of European languages, the shaping of the education system, and the portrayal of culture in the media—all of which have often excluded or undervalued Mizrahi and Sephardic heritage. This cultural dominance has reinforced a social hierarchy that favors Ashkenazi Jews, affecting everything from political power to social norms. The lack of representation in leadership positions further perpetuates this inequality, as decision-making power remains concentrated in the hands of those who belong to the European-descended elite.

Despite these challenges, the struggle for equality and representation has continued, with social movements and advocacy groups working tirelessly to address the discrimination faced by non-European Jewish communities. Over the years, there have been notable efforts to increase awareness of the issues facing Mizrahi and Sephardic Jews, and to push for greater inclusion and representation in all areas of Israeli society. This chapter also explores recent developments that indicate progress, including increased representation in politics and greater recognition of Mizrahi and Sephardic cultural contributions. These efforts, while still ongoing, reflect the resilience of these communities and their determination to achieve equality and full inclusion in Israeli society.

# Mizrahi and Sephardic Jews: A Distinct Identity and Struggle

## HISTORICAL CONTEXT of Mizrahi and Sephardic Migration to Israel

Mizrahi and Sephardic Jews, who hail from Middle Eastern, North African, and Iberian backgrounds, have a distinct identity and history that sets them apart from the predominantly European Ashkenazi Jews who were instrumental in establishing the state of Israel. The migration of Mizrahi Jews to Israel began in large numbers following the establishment of the state in 1948, largely as a result of growing tensions and anti-Jewish sentiment in Arab countries. For Sephardic Jews, who had settled in North Africa and the Ottoman Empire after being expelled from Spain and Portugal during the Inquisition, the creation of Israel provided an opportunity to return to the Jewish homeland, but their migration also involved significant challenges.

Upon arriving in Israel, Mizrahi and Sephardic Jews faced a society that was heavily influenced by European culture and dominated by Ashkenazi leaders who largely held the reins of political power. The early Zionist movement was primarily a European project, and its leaders viewed the incoming Jews from Arab and Muslim countries as culturally backward and in need of modernization. As a result, many Mizrahi and Sephardic Jews were settled in development towns—often in remote and underdeveloped areas of the country—where they faced limited economic opportunities and poor living conditions. The housing policies that placed them in these peripheral areas contributed to the marginalization of Mizrahi and Sephardic communities, isolating them from the social and economic centers of Israeli society.

This marginalization was compounded by the state's assimilationist policies, which pressured Mizrahi and Sephardic Jews to abandon their traditional customs, languages, and identities in favor of the dominant

Ashkenazi culture. The expectation that they would assimilate into a Europeanized version of Israeli society created a sense of alienation among many Mizrahi and Sephardic immigrants, who found themselves torn between preserving their heritage and trying to fit into a society that often regarded their culture as inferior. This struggle for acceptance and equality has been a defining aspect of the Mizrahi and Sephardic experience in Israel.

**Cultural Contributions and Challenges Faced in Israel**

Despite the challenges they faced, Mizrahi and Sephardic Jews have made significant cultural contributions to Israeli society. Their rich traditions, which include music, cuisine, religious practices, and community structures, have added depth and diversity to the cultural fabric of the country. Mizrahi music, with its distinctive Middle Eastern rhythms and melodies, has gained popularity across Israel, influencing mainstream Israeli music and helping to reshape national cultural identity. Traditional foods, such as couscous, shakshuka, and kubeh, have become staples of Israeli cuisine, and the influence of Mizrahi and Sephardic culinary practices is evident in the diverse food culture that characterizes modern Israel.

Religiously, Mizrahi and Sephardic Jews brought with them a unique set of customs and practices that differed from those of the Ashkenazi community. Their approach to Judaism is often characterized by a more relaxed and inclusive attitude, which has helped to shape the broader spectrum of Jewish religious life in Israel. The preservation of Sephardic liturgical traditions and the influence of revered rabbis from the Mizrahi community have contributed to the spiritual diversity of Israeli Judaism, providing an alternative to the more rigid interpretations that sometimes dominate Ashkenazi religious life.

However, the cultural contributions of Mizrahi and Sephardic Jews have often been overshadowed by the systemic discrimination and social exclusion they have faced. The dominance of Ashkenazi culture in Israeli society has meant that Mizrahi and Sephardic traditions have frequently been marginalized or viewed as less sophisticated. This cultural hierarchy has been reinforced through the education system, where Ashkenazi history and culture have been given prominence, while the histories and contributions of Jews from Arab and Muslim countries have been largely ignored or downplayed. As a result, many young Mizrahi and Sephardic Jews have grown up with limited knowledge of their own heritage, contributing to a sense of cultural erasure.

The socioeconomic challenges faced by Mizrahi and Sephardic Jews are also a reflection of the systemic discrimination they have encountered. Many of the development towns to which they were assigned upon arrival remain economically disadvantaged, with limited access to quality education, healthcare, and employment opportunities. The generational impact of these policies has resulted in ongoing disparities between Mizrahi and Ashkenazi Jews, with Mizrahi communities experiencing higher rates of poverty, lower levels of educational attainment, and reduced access to political power. The lack of representation in key decision-making bodies has further exacerbated their marginalization, as policies and priorities are often set without their input or consideration of their unique needs.

In recent decades, there has been a growing movement among Mizrahi and Sephardic Jews to reclaim their cultural heritage and demand greater equality within Israeli society. Activists and cultural figures from these communities have worked to challenge the dominant narrative that privileges Ashkenazi culture, highlighting the contributions of Mizrahi and Sephardic Jews to the development of the state and advocating for recognition of their rights. This has included efforts to reform the education system to include more content about the history and culture of Jews from Arab and Muslim countries, as well as initiatives aimed at increasing political representation and addressing economic disparities.

The struggle of Mizrahi and Sephardic Jews to find their place in Israeli society reflects broader themes of identity, integration, and equality. Their distinct identity, shaped by centuries of life in the Middle East and North Africa, has enriched Israeli culture in countless ways, yet their contributions have often been undervalued or ignored. Addressing the challenges faced by Mizrahi and Sephardic Jews requires not only policy changes to promote social and economic equality but also a broader shift in cultural attitudes to embrace the diversity that is at the heart of Israeli society. Their story is a reminder of the complexities of nation-building in a diverse society and the importance of recognizing and valuing all cultural contributions in creating a truly inclusive national identity.

# Discrimination and Socioeconomic Disparities in Modern Israel

## EMPLOYMENT AND INCOME Disparities Between Ashkenazi and Mizrahi Jews

The socioeconomic disparities between Ashkenazi and Mizrahi Jews are a significant feature of modern Israeli society, rooted in historical discrimination and unequal opportunities that have persisted since the establishment of the state. Mizrahi Jews, who migrated to Israel from Middle Eastern and North African countries, were often viewed by the predominantly Ashkenazi leadership as culturally inferior and in need of assimilation. This perception influenced their initial placement in the socioeconomic hierarchy and continues to impact their opportunities and outcomes today.

One of the most visible manifestations of this inequality is the disparity in employment and income between Ashkenazi and Mizrahi Jews. From the early years of the state, Mizrahi Jews were often assigned to lower-paying, manual labor jobs, while Ashkenazi Jews were more likely to hold positions in administration, education, and other professional fields. This division was partly a result of the state's assimilation policies, which prioritized the skills and experiences of European immigrants while disregarding those of Mizrahi Jews. Over time, this initial gap in employment opportunities has contributed to persistent income inequality, with Mizrahi Jews consistently earning lower average wages compared to their Ashkenazi counterparts.

The employment disparity is also reflected in educational attainment, which has a direct impact on income potential. Mizrahi Jews have historically had less access to quality education, partly due to their placement in underdeveloped towns and neighborhoods with limited educational resources. While progress has been made in closing the education gap, differences in school funding, teacher quality, and access to higher education still exist, contributing to ongoing disparities in employment and income. The result is a cycle of inequality in which lower educational attainment limits access to higher-paying jobs, perpetuating economic disadvantage for Mizrahi families across generations.

Moreover, discrimination in the labor market has further exacerbated these disparities. Studies have shown that Mizrahi Jews are often paid less than Ashkenazi Jews for the same work, and they are less likely to be promoted to senior positions. This discrimination is partly a result of the stereotypes that persist regarding Mizrahi culture and capabilities, which have led to biases in hiring and promotion practices. The underrepresentation of Mizrahi Jews in high-status professions, such as law, medicine, and academia, reflects the broader challenges they face in overcoming these entrenched prejudices.

**Representation in Politics and Government Institutions**

The disparities between Ashkenazi and Mizrahi Jews are not limited to employment and income; they are also evident in the realm of political representation and participation in government institutions. From the early years of the state, the political landscape of Israel was dominated by Ashkenazi leaders who held key positions in government, the military, and other state institutions. This dominance was a result of the Ashkenazi-led Zionist movement, which established the foundations of the state and shaped its political institutions to reflect their values and priorities.

Mizrahi Jews, on the other hand, were largely excluded from positions of power and influence. They were underrepresented in the Knesset (Israel's parliament) and in government ministries, which meant that their voices and interests were often not reflected in national policy decisions. The lack of political representation contributed to the marginalization of Mizrahi communities, as their needs—such as improved housing, education, and economic opportunities—were not adequately addressed by the state. This exclusion from the political process further deepened the socioeconomic disparities between Ashkenazi and Mizrahi Jews, as policies were often crafted without consideration for the unique challenges faced by the latter group.

Over time, there have been efforts to increase the political representation of Mizrahi Jews, and some progress has been made. The rise of political parties that specifically represent the interests of Mizrahi and other marginalized communities, such as Shas, has provided a platform for advocating for their rights and addressing issues of discrimination and inequality. Shas, a religious party with a predominantly Mizrahi base, has played an important role in Israeli politics, particularly in pushing for greater funding for education and social services in disadvantaged communities. However, despite these efforts, Mizrahi Jews remain underrepresented in senior government positions, and the political power they have gained has not always translated into meaningful change in terms of closing the socioeconomic gap.

The military, which plays a central role in Israeli society, has also been a space where disparities in representation have persisted. While many Mizrahi Jews serve in the Israel Defense Forces (IDF), they are less likely to reach the upper echelons of military leadership compared to their Ashkenazi counterparts. The IDF has traditionally been seen as a pathway to social mobility, but the underrepresentation of Mizrahi Jews in senior ranks limits their access to the social and economic benefits that come with military service. This lack of representation in the military hierarchy is another reflection of the broader disparities that exist in Israeli society, where opportunities for advancement are often limited by cultural and systemic biases.

The cultural dominance of Ashkenazi Jews within Israeli institutions has also played a role in perpetuating these disparities. The political and cultural elite in Israel has historically been composed of Ashkenazi Jews, who have shaped the narrative of Israeli identity and defined the norms of political and social life. This has often meant that the experiences and contributions of Mizrahi Jews have been marginalized or ignored, and their cultural identity has been viewed as less legitimate or valuable. The lack of representation in politics and government institutions has meant that Mizrahi Jews have had to fight for recognition and equality in a system that was not designed to accommodate their needs or reflect their identity.

Addressing the discrimination and socioeconomic disparities faced by Mizrahi Jews in modern Israel requires a concerted effort to ensure equal opportunities in education, employment, and political representation. This includes tackling biases in hiring and promotion practices, providing targeted support for disadvantaged communities, and ensuring that the voices of Mizrahi Jews are heard and represented in decision-making processes. It also requires a shift in cultural attitudes to recognize and value the contributions of Mizrahi Jews to Israeli society and to challenge the stereotypes and prejudices that have contributed to their marginalization.

The struggle for equality and representation is an ongoing one, but it is essential for building a more inclusive and just society in which all communities have the opportunity to thrive. The disparities between Ashkenazi and Mizrahi Jews are a reflection of broader issues of social inequality that must be addressed if Israel is to fulfill its promise as a homeland for all Jews, regardless of their origin.

# European-Ashkenazi Dominance in Politics, Culture, and Society

## CULTURAL HEGEMONY: The Role of Language, Education, and Media

Since the establishment of Israel, European-Ashkenazi Jews have held a dominant position in defining the nation's culture and identity. This dominance has been established and maintained through the use of language, education, and media, effectively creating a cultural hegemony that prioritizes Ashkenazi norms while marginalizing the traditions and contributions of other Jewish communities, particularly those from Middle Eastern, North African, and Ethiopian backgrounds.

Language has played a central role in establishing this cultural hegemony. Modern Hebrew, as it was revived and standardized by European Jews, became the unifying national language of Israel, but it was heavily influenced by Ashkenazi linguistic patterns and norms. The focus on Ashkenazi Hebrew marginalized other languages spoken by Jews who immigrated to Israel, including Arabic, Ladino, and Yiddish. For Mizrahi Jews, whose native language was often Arabic, this emphasis on Hebrew came with the expectation that they abandon their linguistic heritage to fully assimilate into Israeli society. This process of linguistic assimilation was part of a broader attempt to create a unified national identity, but it came at the cost of erasing the cultural diversity of Jewish communities.

The education system has also played a key role in promoting Ashkenazi cultural dominance. In the early years of the state, the curriculum was designed primarily by European Jews, with a focus on European Jewish history, the Holocaust, and the Zionist movement's roots in Europe. This curriculum largely ignored the history, culture, and experiences of Jews from Arab and Muslim countries, creating a cultural hierarchy in which Ashkenazi narratives were seen as the standard while those of Mizrahi, Sephardic, and Ethiopian Jews were marginalized. As a result, many young Mizrahi and Sephardic Jews grew up with limited knowledge of their own heritage, which contributed to a sense of cultural inferiority and alienation.

Media has further reinforced the cultural dominance of Ashkenazi Jews. In the early decades of the state, most television, radio, and newspaper content was produced by and for Ashkenazi audiences. The portrayal of Mizrahi and Sephardic Jews in the media was often based on stereotypes that depicted them as uneducated, traditional, or even primitive. These negative representations reinforced societal prejudices and contributed to the marginalization of Mizrahi culture. Although there have been efforts to increase representation and diversify media content in recent years, the legacy of Ashkenazi dominance continues to shape the portrayal of different communities within Israeli society. The media still tends to elevate Ashkenazi cultural norms, making it challenging for other Jewish communities to see their own experiences reflected in the national narrative.

**Political Power and Representation Disparities**

The political landscape of Israel has also been characterized by a disparity in power and representation between Ashkenazi and Mizrahi Jews. From the founding of the state, Ashkenazi Jews occupied most of the key positions in government, the military, and other state institutions. This dominance was a direct result of the Ashkenazi-led Zionist movement, which established the foundations of the state and designed its political and administrative structures. The influence of Ashkenazi leaders on the early development of the state meant that political power and decision-making processes were concentrated in their hands, often to the exclusion of Mizrahi and other marginalized communities.

This unequal representation in politics had significant consequences for the distribution of resources and opportunities within Israeli society. Ashkenazi leaders were more likely to prioritize the needs of their own communities, leading to policies that favored the development of predominantly Ashkenazi areas while neglecting the needs of Mizrahi communities. Many Mizrahi Jews were settled in underdeveloped peripheral towns with limited infrastructure and resources, which hindered their social and economic advancement. The lack of political representation for Mizrahi Jews meant that their voices were not heard in the decision-making processes that shaped national policies, further entrenching the inequalities between different Jewish communities.

The disparity in political representation is also evident in the military, which plays a central role in Israeli society and is often seen as a pathway to social mobility. While many Mizrahi Jews serve in the Israel Defense Forces (IDF), they have historically been underrepresented in the upper ranks of military leadership. The senior ranks of the IDF have traditionally been dominated by officers from elite Ashkenazi backgrounds, limiting the opportunities for Mizrahi soldiers to advance and benefit from the social and economic advantages that come with military service. This underrepresentation in the military hierarchy reflects the broader patterns of inequality that exist within Israeli society, where opportunities for advancement are often limited by cultural and systemic biases.

In recent decades, there have been efforts to address the disparities in political representation, and some progress has been made. The rise of political parties that specifically represent the interests of Mizrahi and Sephardic Jews, such as Shas, has provided a platform for these communities to advocate for their rights and challenge the dominance of the Ashkenazi elite. Shas, a religious party with a predominantly Mizrahi base, has been successful in securing representation in the Knesset and influencing government policy, particularly in areas related to education and social welfare. However, despite these efforts, Mizrahi Jews remain underrepresented in the highest levels of government, and the political power they have gained has not always translated into meaningful change in terms of closing the socioeconomic gap.

The judiciary, another important institution in Israeli society, has also been dominated by Ashkenazi Jews. The underrepresentation of Mizrahi judges in the courts has contributed to a lack of trust in the legal system among many in the Mizrahi community, who feel that their interests are not adequately represented or protected by the state. The judiciary plays a crucial role in shaping the legal framework of the state and ensuring that the rights of all citizens are upheld, and increasing the diversity of the judiciary is essential for building a more inclusive and equitable legal system.

The European-Ashkenazi dominance in politics, culture, and society has created a hierarchy that has marginalized the experiences and contributions of Mizrahi, Sephardic, and Ethiopian Jews. This dominance has been maintained through cultural hegemony in language, education, and media, as well as disparities in political power and representation. Addressing these inequalities requires not only increasing representation for marginalized communities but also a broader shift in cultural attitudes to recognize and value the diverse contributions of all Jewish communities to the fabric of Israeli society.

# The Ongoing Struggle for Equality and Representation

**SOCIAL MOVEMENTS ADDRESSING Discrimination**

The struggle for equality and representation among Mizrahi and Sephardic Jews in Israel has been an ongoing effort, driven by social movements and activism that seek to challenge the discrimination and marginalization faced by these communities. From the early years of the state, Mizrahi Jews found themselves at a disadvantage, often settled in underdeveloped towns with limited access to education, employment, and other opportunities. This marginalization led to the emergence of social movements that aimed to address the injustices faced by Mizrahi Jews and demand equal treatment.

One of the most prominent movements addressing discrimination against Mizrahi Jews was the Israeli Black Panthers, formed in the early 1970s by a group of young Mizrahi activists in Jerusalem. Inspired by the Black Panther movement in the United States, the Israeli Black Panthers sought to draw attention to the socioeconomic disparities between Ashkenazi and Mizrahi Jews and to protest the state's discriminatory policies. Through demonstrations, protests, and direct action, the movement highlighted issues such as poverty, lack of housing, and educational inequality, bringing the plight of Mizrahi Jews to the forefront of the national conversation. While the movement faced significant opposition from the government, it succeeded in raising awareness of the discrimination faced by Mizrahi Jews and laid the groundwork for future efforts to address inequality.

Religious parties, such as Shas, have also played a significant role in advocating for the rights of Mizrahi Jews and challenging the dominance of the Ashkenazi elite in Israeli society. Founded in the 1980s, Shas emerged as a political force that represented the interests of the Mizrahi community, particularly in the areas of education and social welfare. The party has been successful in securing government funding for religious schools that cater to Mizrahi students and in pushing for policies that address the needs of disadvantaged communities. By providing a platform for Mizrahi voices in the political arena, Shas has helped to increase the visibility of the issues facing the community and has been instrumental in promoting greater representation for Mizrahi Jews in Israeli politics.

In recent years, grassroots organizations and cultural initiatives have also played a role in addressing discrimination and promoting equality for Mizrahi and Sephardic Jews. These organizations work to preserve and celebrate Mizrahi culture, challenge stereotypes, and create opportunities for economic and social advancement. By focusing on education, community empowerment, and cultural pride, these initiatives aim to counter the historical marginalization of Mizrahi Jews and to build a more inclusive society in which all communities are valued and respected.

**Recent Developments in Representation and Inclusion**

There have been notable developments in recent years that reflect progress in the struggle for equality and representation for Mizrahi and Sephardic Jews. Increased political representation, greater visibility in cultural spaces, and efforts to address socioeconomic disparities have all contributed to a gradual shift in the status of Mizrahi and Sephardic communities within Israeli society. While challenges remain, these developments represent important steps toward greater inclusion and equality.

In the political arena, there has been an increase in the representation of Mizrahi and Sephardic Jews in the Knesset and in government ministries. Political parties that represent the interests of these communities, such as Shas, have gained influence and have been able to advocate for policies that address the needs of Mizrahi Jews. In addition, Mizrahi politicians have risen to prominent positions within mainstream political parties, further increasing the visibility of Mizrahi voices in national decision-making processes. This increased representation has allowed for greater attention to be paid to issues such as housing, education, and social welfare, which disproportionately affect Mizrahi communities.

Culturally, there has also been a growing recognition of the contributions of Mizrahi and Sephardic Jews to Israeli society. Mizrahi music, food, and traditions have gained greater visibility and acceptance in the mainstream, challenging the dominance of Ashkenazi culture. Artists, writers, and musicians from Mizrahi backgrounds have played a key role in reshaping the cultural narrative, highlighting the richness and diversity of Mizrahi heritage and pushing for a more inclusive understanding of Israeli identity. The increased presence of Mizrahi culture in media, literature, and the arts has helped to counter stereotypes and promote a more nuanced view of the contributions of Mizrahi Jews to the development of the state.

Education has also been a focus of recent efforts to promote inclusion and equality. There has been a push to reform the curriculum to include more content about the history and culture of Mizrahi and Sephardic Jews, providing students with a more comprehensive understanding of the diverse backgrounds that make up Israeli society. By incorporating the experiences and contributions of Mizrahi Jews into the national narrative, these educational reforms aim to foster a greater appreciation for the diversity of Israeli society and to challenge the cultural hierarchy that has historically marginalized Mizrahi communities.

Efforts to address socioeconomic disparities have also seen some progress, with targeted programs aimed at improving access to education, employment, and housing for disadvantaged communities. Government initiatives and nonprofit organizations have worked to provide scholarships for Mizrahi students, vocational training programs, and support for small businesses in underdeveloped areas. These programs are designed to break the cycle of poverty that has affected many Mizrahi families and to create opportunities for social mobility and economic advancement.

While these developments represent important steps forward, the struggle for equality and representation is far from over. Mizrahi and Sephardic Jews continue to face challenges in achieving full equality, and the legacy of discrimination and marginalization remains a significant barrier. The ongoing efforts of social movements, cultural initiatives, and political advocacy are essential in pushing for further change and in ensuring that all communities within Israel have the opportunity to thrive and contribute to the nation's development.

The ongoing struggle for equality and representation for Mizrahi and Sephardic Jews is a testament to the resilience and determination of these communities. Despite the challenges they have faced, they have made significant contributions to the cultural, social, and political fabric of Israeli society. The progress that has been made in recent years offers hope for a more inclusive future, in which the diverse backgrounds and experiences of all Jewish communities are recognized, valued, and celebrated.

# Chapter 7: Western Powers' Support of Israel

Chapter 7 examines the role of Western powers, particularly the United States and European nations, in supporting Israel since its establishment in 1948. This support has been pivotal in shaping Israel's political, economic, and military standing in the region, ensuring its security and fostering its growth as a powerful state in the Middle East. The early diplomatic recognition of Israel by Western powers set the stage for decades of strategic alliances, particularly during the Cold War, when Israel became a crucial ally in a region of vital geopolitical importance. The support of Western countries, motivated by both strategic and ideological factors, has remained a cornerstone of Israel's international relations.

Political backing from Western nations, especially the United States, has been a key factor in shielding Israel from international criticism and pressure. This chapter explores how the use of veto power in the United Nations has been instrumental in blocking resolutions critical of Israel, thereby preventing international accountability for actions such as settlement expansion and military operations in Palestinian territories. In addition to using vetoes, Western powers have exerted diplomatic pressure on international bodies to ensure that Israel is not subjected to sanctions or punitive measures, effectively enabling it to continue its policies without significant repercussions.

Financial and military aid provided by Western powers has further bolstered Israel's position in the region. The United States, in particular, has provided substantial financial assistance, often with specific conditions that align with American strategic interests. This aid has been crucial in funding infrastructure, defense, and economic development. Moreover, the transfer of advanced military technology and equipment has ensured that Israel maintains a qualitative military edge over its neighbors, reinforcing its position as a dominant regional power. These financial and military ties not only strengthen Israel's capabilities but also deepen its reliance on Western support, creating a mutually beneficial relationship that serves the interests of both parties.

The chapter also addresses the role of Western powers in ignoring or downplaying reports of war crimes and human rights violations committed by Israel. Despite numerous allegations and investigations by international organizations, Western nations have often remained silent or dismissed such reports, allowing Israel to continue its actions with little accountability. This silence is compounded by the role of the media in shaping public perception, where narratives favorable to Israel are often amplified, while those highlighting the suffering of Palestinians receive less attention. By examining these aspects of Western support, the chapter reveals the extent to which political, financial, and military backing has enabled Israel's actions and shaped the ongoing conflict in the region.

# Historical Context: The Role of the United States and European Powers

## EARLY DIPLOMATIC RECOGNITION and Support Post-1948

The establishment of the state of Israel in 1948 was met with significant diplomatic support from both the United States and several European powers. This early recognition was crucial for Israel's legitimacy on the international stage and its survival during its formative years. The United States, under President Harry Truman, was one of the first countries to officially recognize Israel, doing so just minutes after the declaration of independence on May 14, 1948. This early recognition provided a crucial boost to Israel, signaling strong American support for the new state at a time when its very existence was under threat from neighboring Arab countries that opposed its creation.

European powers also played a key role in supporting the fledgling state. The United Kingdom, which had previously held the mandate over Palestine, played a complex role in the establishment of Israel. Although Britain officially ended its mandate without directly supporting the declaration of independence, many European countries extended diplomatic recognition to Israel soon afterward, helping to consolidate its status as a legitimate state. France, in particular, became a close ally of Israel in the 1950s, providing significant military and technical assistance that helped Israel develop its defense capabilities. This support from both the United States and European nations was instrumental in ensuring Israel's survival during its early conflicts, such as the 1948 Arab-Israeli War, and in helping it establish itself as a sovereign nation.

The early diplomatic support from Western powers was motivated by a variety of factors, including sympathy for the Jewish people following the Holocaust, strategic interests in the Middle East, and a desire to establish a stable ally in a region characterized by political turmoil. The atrocities of World War II had generated significant sympathy for the plight of the Jewish people, and the establishment of Israel was seen by many in the West as a necessary response to centuries of persecution. At the same time, Western powers were also motivated by their own strategic considerations, recognizing the potential value of a friendly state in the Middle East, particularly as the region's geopolitical importance grew with the discovery and development of oil resources.

### The Cold War Era and Strategic Alliances

The relationship between Israel and the United States, as well as other Western powers, deepened significantly during the Cold War era. The geopolitical dynamics of the Cold War, in which the United States and the Soviet Union competed for influence around the world, had a profound impact on the Middle East, and Israel emerged as a key ally for the West in this strategic contest. The United States saw Israel as a bulwark against Soviet influence in the region, particularly as several Arab states, such as Egypt and Syria, began to align themselves with the Soviet Union and adopt socialist policies. This alignment with the Soviet bloc made Israel's strategic importance to the United States even more pronounced.

In response, the United States began to provide Israel with substantial military and economic support, which would become a cornerstone of the bilateral relationship. In the 1960s, American aid to Israel increased significantly, especially after the Six-Day War in 1967, when Israel's military victory over its Arab neighbors demonstrated its potential as a strong and reliable ally. The United States began supplying Israel with advanced weaponry, which not only helped ensure Israel's military superiority in the region but also tied the two countries closer together in terms of strategic cooperation. This support was formalized with the signing of numerous agreements, and by the 1970s, the United States had become Israel's primary supplier of military aid and its most important diplomatic ally.

European powers also played a significant role during the Cold War in supporting Israel, albeit with some variations in their approach. France was a crucial ally in the 1950s and 1960s, providing Israel with both military hardware and assistance in developing its nuclear program. The Franco-Israeli alliance was particularly strong during the Suez Crisis in 1956, when Israel, along with France and the United Kingdom, launched a military campaign against Egypt in response to President Gamal Abdel Nasser's nationalization of the Suez Canal. This cooperation highlighted the shared strategic interests of Israel and certain European powers during the early Cold War years.

However, the relationship between Israel and European countries began to change in the late 1960s and 1970s, as European governments increasingly sought to balance their ties with Israel against their growing interests in the Arab world. The Arab oil embargo of 1973, which was imposed in response to Western support for Israel during the Yom Kippur War, highlighted the economic and political leverage that Arab states could wield. As a result, many European countries began to adopt a more neutral stance in the Israeli-Arab conflict, seeking to maintain good relations with both sides. Despite this shift, European powers continued to provide Israel with diplomatic and economic support, albeit less overtly than during the earlier years of the Cold War.

The Cold War also saw the emergence of strategic alliances that shaped the regional balance of power and further solidified Israel's relationship with the West. In addition to military aid and diplomatic backing, the United States provided Israel with economic assistance that helped spur its economic development and technological innovation. The strategic partnership between the two countries deepened further after the 1979 Iranian Revolution, which led to the loss of a key American ally in the region. With Iran now aligned against

Western interests, Israel's role as a strategic partner to the United States became even more important, and the relationship between the two countries continued to evolve into one of the closest alliances in the world.

The role of the United States and European powers in supporting Israel during its early years and throughout the Cold War was instrumental in shaping the geopolitical landscape of the Middle East. The strategic alliances that developed during this period ensured Israel's military and economic strength, allowing it to maintain its security in a hostile region. At the same time, the support from Western powers also contributed to the complexities of the Israeli-Arab conflict, as it deepened divisions between Israel and its neighbors and fueled tensions that continue to this day. The historical context of this support provides important insights into the ongoing dynamics of the Middle East and the role that external powers have played in shaping the region's conflicts and alliances.

# Political Backing: Vetoes and Diplomatic Maneuvers to Shield Israel

## USE OF VETO POWER IN the United Nations

The United States has consistently used its veto power in the United Nations Security Council to shield Israel from international criticism and to prevent resolutions that could undermine Israel's interests. Since the 1970s, the United States has cast numerous vetoes on resolutions that condemned Israeli actions, including those related to settlement expansion, military operations, and human rights violations in the occupied Palestinian territories. These vetoes have often been cast in response to resolutions that the United States deemed to be biased against Israel or that threatened to impose measures such as sanctions or international investigations.

The use of the veto has been a powerful tool in ensuring that Israel is not subjected to punitive measures by the international community. By preventing the passage of resolutions critical of Israel, the United States has effectively blocked the UN from taking any significant action that could pressure Israel to change its policies toward the Palestinians. This consistent use of the veto has also signaled to Israel that it can count on American diplomatic support, even in the face of widespread international condemnation.

One of the most notable examples of the use of the veto to protect Israel was during the 2004 resolution condemning Israel's construction of the separation barrier in the West Bank. The barrier, which Israel argued was necessary for security reasons, was widely criticized as a means of annexing Palestinian land and altering the demographic balance in favor of Israeli settlers. Despite widespread support for the resolution, the United States vetoed it, citing concerns that it did not adequately address Israel's legitimate security needs. This action demonstrated the United States' willingness to use its influence to shield Israel from international scrutiny, even when its actions were viewed by much of the world as a violation of international law.

The repeated use of the veto has not only protected Israel from potential consequences but has also contributed to a perception of bias in the UN, leading many countries to view the United States as an obstacle to a fair resolution of the Israeli-Palestinian conflict. This perception has had a lasting impact on the credibility of the UN as a forum for addressing the conflict, with many Palestinians and their supporters arguing that the international community has been unable to hold Israel accountable for its actions due to American intervention.

**Diplomatic Pressure on International Bodies**

In addition to using its veto power at the United Nations, the United States has also exerted significant diplomatic pressure on international bodies to shield Israel from criticism and to ensure that it is not subjected to punitive measures. This pressure has taken various forms, including lobbying efforts, financial leverage, and behind-the-scenes negotiations to influence the actions and decisions of international organizations.

One of the key arenas where the United States has used diplomatic pressure to protect Israel is the United Nations Human Rights Council (UNHRC). The UNHRC has frequently criticized Israel for its treatment of Palestinians and its actions in the occupied territories, leading the United States to accuse the council of having an anti-Israel bias. In response, the United States has often lobbied other member states to prevent resolutions critical of Israel from being adopted and has even withdrawn from the council altogether, as it did in 2018, citing its perceived bias against Israel. By leveraging its influence within the UNHRC, the United States has sought to limit the council's ability to take meaningful action against Israel and to ensure that any criticism of Israeli policies is minimized.

The United States has also used its diplomatic clout to influence the actions of the International Criminal Court (ICC) in relation to

Israel. When the ICC announced that it would open an investigation into alleged war crimes committed by both Israel and Palestinian armed groups in the occupied territories, the United States publicly opposed the investigation and pressured the court to drop the case. The U.S. government argued that the ICC did not have jurisdiction over the matter, as Israel is not a party to the Rome Statute, and warned that the investigation could have negative consequences for the peace process. By taking this stance, the United States effectively shielded Israel from potential legal consequences for its actions in the occupied territories.

Financial leverage has also been a key tool in exerting diplomatic pressure on international bodies. The United States is one of the largest contributors to the UN and other international organizations, and it has occasionally used the threat of withholding funding as a means of influencing decisions related to Israel. For example, in 2011, when UNESCO admitted Palestine as a full member, the United States cut its funding to the organization, leading to a significant budget shortfall. This action was intended to signal American disapproval of any moves that could be seen as legitimizing Palestinian statehood outside of a negotiated agreement with Israel. By using its financial contributions as leverage, the United States has sought to ensure that international organizations align their actions with American—and by extension, Israeli—interests.

The United States' diplomatic efforts to protect Israel have extended beyond formal international organizations to include bilateral relations with other countries. American diplomats have frequently lobbied allied nations to oppose or abstain from voting on resolutions critical of Israel, both at the UN and in other international forums. These efforts have often been successful in limiting the level of international support for resolutions condemning Israel, ensuring that any such measures lack the broad consensus needed to carry significant weight.

The political backing provided by the United States through vetoes and diplomatic maneuvers has been instrumental in shielding Israel from international criticism and consequences for its actions. This support has allowed Israel to continue its policies in the occupied territories without fear of punitive measures from the international community, reinforcing its position in the region. However, it has also contributed to a perception of bias and double standards, undermining the credibility of international institutions and complicating efforts to achieve a just and lasting resolution to the Israeli-Palestinian conflict.

# Financial and Military Aid: The Economic Support Sustaining Israel

## U.S. FINANCIAL AID Packages and Their Conditions

Since the establishment of the state of Israel, the United States has been its largest and most consistent provider of financial aid. This aid, which has totaled more than $150 billion since 1948, has played a critical role in sustaining Israel's economy and ensuring its security. The financial support provided by the U.S. comes in the form of annual aid packages, with a significant portion allocated for military purposes and the rest for economic support and development projects. The aid is intended to bolster Israel's ability to defend itself against regional threats, maintain military superiority, and support its economic growth.

One of the most notable aid agreements is the Memorandum of Understanding (MOU) signed between the United States and Israel, which outlines the terms and conditions of American assistance. The most recent MOU, signed in 2016, provides Israel with $38 billion in military aid over a ten-year period, making it the largest aid package the United States has ever provided to any country. This agreement includes $33 billion in Foreign Military Financing (FMF), which allows Israel to purchase advanced U.S. military equipment, and $5 billion for missile defense programs. The MOU reflects the strategic partnership between the two countries and underscores America's commitment to Israel's security.

Unlike most other recipients of U.S. aid, Israel is granted unique conditions regarding how the aid is used. A significant portion of the military aid provided to Israel—up to 26%—can be spent on procurement from Israeli defense contractors, rather than requiring the entire sum to be spent on American-made goods and services. This arrangement has helped to strengthen Israel's domestic defense industry and has contributed to the development of cutting-edge military technologies. The special conditions attached to U.S. aid underscore the close relationship between the two countries and the importance placed on ensuring that Israel remains a regional military power.

However, U.S. aid to Israel also comes with conditions that influence Israeli policies and actions. While the aid is intended to support Israel's security, it also serves as a tool for the United States to exert influence over Israeli decision-making. For example, during the 1980s, the United States used the withholding of financial aid as leverage to pressure Israel into halting the construction of new settlements in the West Bank. Although such measures have been used sparingly, the potential withholding of aid remains a tool that American policymakers can use to influence Israeli actions, particularly when it comes to issues that may impact the prospects for peace with the Palestinians.

The economic support provided by the United States has had a significant impact on Israel's development, enabling it to become one of the most technologically advanced and economically stable countries in the region. U.S. aid has helped to fund infrastructure projects, research and development, and other initiatives that have contributed to Israel's economic growth. This financial assistance has not only strengthened Israel's military capabilities but has also supported its broader economic objectives, allowing it to maintain a high standard of living for its citizens despite the challenges posed by regional instability.

**Military Assistance and Technology Transfers**

In addition to financial aid, the United States has provided Israel with extensive military assistance, including advanced weaponry, training, and technology transfers. This military support has been a cornerstone of the U.S.-Israel relationship, ensuring that Israel maintains a qualitative military edge (QME) over its neighbors. The concept of QME is a key element of U.S. policy, aimed at ensuring that

Israel has the capability to defend itself effectively against any potential threats, particularly from hostile regional actors.

The United States has supplied Israel with a wide range of advanced military equipment, including fighter jets, tanks, missile defense systems, and precision-guided munitions. One of the most significant aspects of U.S. military assistance is the provision of advanced aircraft, such as the F-35 stealth fighter, which has given Israel a significant technological advantage in the region. The transfer of such advanced technology is intended to ensure that Israel can respond effectively to any potential threats, whether from state actors like Iran or from non-state groups such as Hezbollah and Hamas.

Missile defense has been another major focus of U.S.-Israeli military cooperation. The United States has provided funding and technical support for the development of Israel's missile defense systems, including the Iron Dome, David's Sling, and Arrow programs. These systems are designed to intercept and destroy incoming rockets and missiles, providing a critical layer of protection for Israeli civilians. The Iron Dome, in particular, has proven to be highly effective in intercepting short-range rockets fired from Gaza, significantly reducing casualties and property damage during periods of conflict. U.S. support for these missile defense programs has been instrumental in enhancing Israel's ability to protect itself from external threats and has become a key component of the strategic partnership between the two countries.

Technology transfers between the United States and Israel have also played a crucial role in strengthening Israel's military capabilities. The close collaboration between the defense industries of both countries has led to the development of cutting-edge technologies that have enhanced the capabilities of both the Israeli and American armed forces. For example, Israeli innovations in drone technology, cybersecurity, and intelligence gathering have been shared with the United States, benefiting both countries' defense sectors. This exchange of technology and expertise has not only bolstered Israel's military strength but has also deepened the strategic partnership between the two nations.

The military assistance provided by the United States has allowed Israel to maintain a significant military advantage over its regional adversaries, ensuring its security in a volatile environment. However, this support has also had broader implications for the dynamics of the Middle East. The provision of advanced weaponry and technology to Israel has contributed to an ongoing arms race in the region, with neighboring countries seeking to bolster their own military capabilities in response. This has led to increased tensions and has complicated efforts to achieve a lasting peace in the region.

The financial and military aid provided by the United States has been a key factor in sustaining Israel's security and economic stability. The aid packages, favorable conditions, and military assistance have ensured that Israel remains a dominant military power in the region, capable of defending itself against potential threats. At the same time, this support has deepened the strategic partnership between the two countries, creating a relationship that is characterized by mutual interests and shared values. While the aid has undoubtedly contributed to Israel's strength and resilience, it has also had broader implications for the region, influencing the dynamics of the Israeli-Palestinian conflict and the balance of power in the Middle East.

# Ignoring War Crimes: How Western Powers Enable Israeli Actions

**REPORTS OF WAR CRIMES and Western Silence**

Over the years, numerous reports have emerged accusing Israel of committing war crimes, particularly in its military actions in the occupied Palestinian territories and during conflicts with Gaza. These accusations have been made by reputable international organizations, including the United Nations, Human Rights Watch, and Amnesty International. Reports have documented a range of alleged violations, such as disproportionate use of force, targeting civilian infrastructure, and collective punishment, all of which are considered violations of international humanitarian law.

One notable example is the 2008-2009 Gaza War, also known as Operation Cast Lead, during which Israel's military actions were widely condemned for their impact on civilians. The UN's Goldstone Report concluded that both Israel and Palestinian armed groups had committed war crimes, but it particularly highlighted the disproportionate response by Israel and the extensive damage to civilian lives and infrastructure. Despite these findings, Western governments, particularly the United States and several European nations, largely dismissed the report and instead defended Israel's right to self-defense without addressing the allegations of excessive force and violations of international law.

This pattern of silence or outright dismissal has been repeated in subsequent conflicts, including the 2014 Gaza War (Operation Protective Edge) and the more recent escalations in Gaza. Reports of bombings of residential buildings, schools, and medical facilities have drawn widespread international condemnation, but Western powers have often shielded Israel from accountability by blocking or voting against resolutions that seek to investigate or impose consequences for these actions. The United States, in particular, has used its diplomatic influence to prevent international bodies from taking punitive action, arguing that Israel's actions are justified responses to threats from militant groups.

This consistent refusal to hold Israel accountable for alleged war crimes sends a clear message that it can act with impunity. The lack of meaningful consequences not only undermines the credibility of international law but also perpetuates a cycle of violence in which both sides feel justified in their actions. For Palestinians, the failure of the international community to respond to their suffering creates deep resentment and a sense of injustice, while for Israel, the lack of accountability reinforces the belief that its actions are necessary and legitimate.

### The Role of Media in Shaping Public Perception

The role of the media in shaping public perception of the Israeli-Palestinian conflict cannot be understated. Western media outlets, particularly those in the United States and Europe, play a significant role in framing the narrative of the conflict, and their coverage often reflects the biases and interests of their respective governments. The way in which incidents of violence and alleged war crimes are reported can influence public opinion, shaping how audiences understand the causes and consequences of the conflict.

In many Western media outlets, coverage of the Israeli-Palestinian conflict tends to focus on Israel's right to self-defense and the threat posed by militant groups such as Hamas, while downplaying or omitting the experiences and suffering of Palestinian civilians. Reports of Israeli military actions are often framed in the context of a response to rocket attacks, with little attention given to the broader context of occupation, blockade, and systemic human rights abuses faced by Palestinians. This framing creates a perception that Israel is acting defensively, while Palestinian resistance is portrayed as aggression, contributing to a one-sided understanding of the conflict.

When allegations of war crimes are raised, Western media often give disproportionate attention to Israeli government statements and justifications, while the voices of Palestinian victims and international human rights organizations are marginalized. The use of language also plays a significant role in shaping perception; terms such as "clashes" or "conflict" are frequently used to describe situations where there is a significant imbalance of power and casualties, obscuring the reality of the situation. This type of reporting contributes to the normalization of violence against Palestinians and diminishes the urgency of addressing alleged violations of international law.

The media's role in downplaying or ignoring reports of war crimes is further influenced by the strong relationship between Western governments and Israel. Media outlets are often reluctant to publish content that may be seen as too critical of Israel, fearing backlash from powerful political lobbies and interest groups. This has led to self-censorship and a lack of investigative journalism on issues related to Israeli actions in the occupied territories. As a result, Western audiences are often unaware of the full extent of the human rights abuses taking place, and there is limited public pressure on governments to hold Israel accountable.

The consequence of this skewed media coverage is that the narrative surrounding the Israeli-Palestinian conflict is heavily influenced by the perspective of Western powers, which often aligns with Israel's interests. This has a direct impact on the policy decisions of Western governments, as public opinion plays a crucial role in shaping foreign policy. When the media fails to accurately report on allegations of war crimes and the humanitarian impact of Israeli actions, it becomes easier for Western governments to justify their continued support for Israel and to ignore calls for accountability.

The failure of Western powers to address reports of war crimes, coupled with the role of the media in shaping public perception, has enabled Israel to continue its actions in the occupied territories with little fear of repercussions. This dynamic not only perpetuates the suffering of Palestinians but also undermines the principles of international law and human rights. Addressing this issue requires a more balanced and critical approach from both the media and Western governments, one that holds all parties accountable for their actions and seeks a just and lasting resolution to the conflict.

# List of Alleged Israeli War Crimes and Detailed Accounts

**OPERATION CAST LEAD (2008-2009)**

Operation Cast Lead, also known as the 2008-2009 Gaza War, resulted in a significant number of civilian casualties and extensive destruction in Gaza. Numerous international organizations, including the United Nations, Human Rights Watch, and Amnesty International, accused Israel of committing war crimes during this operation.

**Disproportionate Use of Force:** The Israeli military's use of disproportionate force was one of the main accusations during Operation Cast Lead. Israel's heavy bombardment of densely populated civilian areas led to the deaths of over 1,400 Palestinians, more than half of whom were civilians, including hundreds of children. The use of artillery shells and airstrikes in residential areas violated the principle of proportionality under international humanitarian law, which requires military actions to minimize harm to civilians.

**Use of White Phosphorus:** Israel's use of white phosphorus munitions in civilian areas during Operation Cast Lead was widely condemned as a war crime. White phosphorus is a highly incendiary substance that can cause severe burns and is meant to be used as a smokescreen or to mark targets. However, in Gaza, it was used in residential areas, leading to severe injuries and deaths among civilians. Human Rights Watch documented instances where white phosphorus shells were fired over crowded neighborhoods, resulting in casualties and the destruction of civilian infrastructure, including schools and hospitals.

**Targeting of Civilian Infrastructure:** During the operation, Israeli forces targeted critical civilian infrastructure, including schools, hospitals, and government buildings. One of the most infamous incidents was the bombing of the United Nations Relief and Works Agency (UNRWA) compound in Gaza City, which was sheltering hundreds of civilians at the time. The attack resulted in injuries and further displacement of already vulnerable people. Under international law, the targeting of civilian infrastructure is prohibited unless it is being used for military purposes, and there was no evidence to suggest that these sites posed a military threat.

### Operation Protective Edge (2014)

Operation Protective Edge, launched in 2014, was one of the deadliest conflicts between Israel and Hamas. The war led to over 2,200 Palestinian deaths, the majority of whom were civilians, and widespread destruction of homes and infrastructure in Gaza.

**Indiscriminate Bombardment:** One of the key allegations against Israel during Operation Protective Edge was the use of indiscriminate bombardment. Israeli forces carried out extensive aerial, naval, and ground attacks on Gaza, which is one of the most densely populated areas in the world. Entire neighborhoods, such as Shuja'iyya, were flattened, and thousands of homes were destroyed. The scale of the destruction and the number of civilian casualties led to accusations that Israel had failed to distinguish between military targets and civilians, in violation of international law.

**Targeting of UN Shelters:** During the conflict, Israeli forces targeted several UN-designated shelters where civilians had taken refuge. For example, an attack on an UNRWA school in Jabalia, which was being used as a shelter, resulted in the deaths of at least 16 civilians and injuries to over 100 others. The UN had provided the coordinates of these shelters to the Israeli military to avoid attacks, yet they were still targeted. The intentional or reckless targeting of civilians or civilian shelters is considered a war crime under international law.

**Killing of Fleeing Civilians:** Reports emerged that Israeli forces killed civilians who were attempting to flee areas of intense fighting. Human Rights Watch documented cases in which civilians carrying white flags, which are used to signal non-combatant status, were shot and killed by Israeli forces. Targeting civilians who are clearly not engaged in hostilities is a grave breach of the Geneva Conventions and constitutes a war crime.

### Sniper Attacks on Protesters (2018-2019)

During the Great March of Return protests, which began in 2018, thousands of Palestinians gathered near the Gaza-Israel border fence to protest against the blockade of Gaza and demand the right of return for Palestinian refugees. Israeli forces responded to the protests with live ammunition, resulting in the deaths of over 200 Palestinians, including children, medics, and journalists.

**Use of Lethal Force Against Unarmed Protesters:** Israeli snipers used live ammunition against unarmed protesters, many of whom posed no imminent threat to the Israeli forces stationed at the border. The United Nations Independent Commission of Inquiry found that many of those killed were shot while posing no immediate danger, such as children, medics attempting to assist the wounded, and journalists wearing press vests. The use of lethal force against unarmed individuals is considered a violation of international human rights law and can constitute a war crime.

**Targeting of Medical Personnel and Journalists:** During the protests, several medics and journalists were killed or injured by Israeli forces. Rouzan al-Najjar, a 21-year-old volunteer medic, was shot and killed while attempting to treat injured protesters, despite wearing clothing that clearly identified her as medical personnel. Yaser Murtaja, a journalist wearing a vest marked "PRESS," was also shot and killed. Under international law, targeting medical personnel and journalists is strictly prohibited, as they are considered protected persons during armed conflict.

### Blockade of Gaza

The Israeli blockade of Gaza, which has been in place since 2007, has also been described by some as a form of collective punishment, which is prohibited under international law. The blockade severely restricts the movement of people and goods into and out of Gaza, resulting in widespread poverty, unemployment, and a lack of access to essential services.

**Collective Punishment:** The blockade affects nearly every aspect of life in Gaza, from access to medical care to the availability of clean water and electricity. By restricting the movement of goods and people, Israel has created a situation in which the civilian population is deprived of basic necessities. The UN has repeatedly stated that the blockade constitutes collective punishment of the entire population of Gaza, which is a violation of the Fourth Geneva Convention.

**Destruction of Civilian Infrastructure:** Israeli restrictions have also impeded the reconstruction of infrastructure that was destroyed during military operations. For example, building materials such as cement and steel are heavily restricted, which has made it difficult for Palestinians in Gaza to rebuild homes, schools, and hospitals. The destruction of civilian infrastructure, combined with restrictions on rebuilding, has left many Palestinians in a perpetual state of vulnerability.

### West Bank and East Jerusalem

In addition to its actions in Gaza, Israel has been accused of committing war crimes in the West Bank and East Jerusalem, primarily related to the expansion of settlements and the treatment of Palestinian civilians.

**Illegal Settlement Expansion:** The construction of Israeli settlements in the occupied West Bank and East Jerusalem is considered illegal under international law, as it violates the Fourth Geneva Convention, which prohibits an occupying power from transferring its civilian population into the territory it occupies. The expansion of settlements has led to the displacement of Palestinian families and the appropriation of Palestinian land and resources. The International Criminal Court (ICC) has indicated that the expansion of settlements may constitute a war crime, as it involves the transfer of populations and the unlawful appropriation of property.

**Demolition of Homes and Forcible Transfer:** The Israeli military has carried out the demolition of thousands of Palestinian homes in the West Bank, often citing the lack of building permits, which are nearly impossible for Palestinians to obtain. These demolitions have led to the forcible transfer of Palestinian communities, which is considered a violation of the Fourth Geneva Convention. The demolition of homes and the displacement of families contribute to the ongoing fragmentation of Palestinian territories and make it difficult for Palestinians to maintain a cohesive presence in the West Bank.

**Excessive Use of Force and Extrajudicial Killings:** Israeli forces have been accused of using excessive force during operations in the West Bank, including the use of live ammunition against unarmed civilians. There have also been reports of extrajudicial killings of Palestinians suspected of carrying out attacks or posing a threat. The killing of individuals without due process is a violation of international human rights law and can amount to a war crime.

The allegations of war crimes committed by Israel have been the subject of numerous investigations by international organizations, human rights groups, and, more recently, the International Criminal Court. These allegations include the use of disproportionate force, targeting of civilians and civilian infrastructure, collective punishment, and illegal settlement expansion. Addressing these alleged war crimes and ensuring accountability is essential for achieving justice for the victims and for advancing the prospects of a peaceful resolution to the Israeli-Palestinian conflict.

# Chapter 8: Reparations and Accountability

Chapter 8 explores the complex issues of reparations and accountability in the context of Israel and the displacement of Palestinians. At the heart of this discussion is the concept of colonial responsibility—acknowledging the historical injustices committed during the establishment of Israel and examining the ethical implications of these actions. The debate around colonial responsibility involves grappling with questions of moral obligation, historical guilt, and the practicalities of righting past wrongs. Comparisons with other post-colonial contexts, such as reparations efforts in South Africa or compensation to Indigenous communities in various countries, provide insight into how other nations have sought to address their colonial past and offer potential models for Israel and Palestine.

Addressing the displacement of Palestinians is a critical part of the conversation on reparative justice. The Palestinian right of return is a deeply contested issue, both historically and legally, and lies at the core of the broader struggle for Palestinian rights. This chapter examines the historical context of the right of return, its basis in international law, and the challenges that have prevented its realization. Efforts related to property restitution and compensation are also discussed, highlighting the demands of displaced Palestinian families and the obstacles they face in reclaiming their lost homes and land. These issues are essential in understanding the broader quest for justice and recognition of the losses suffered by Palestinians since 1948.

The role of international law and global organizations in addressing these injustices is also critical. Various United Nations resolutions have called for the recognition of Palestinian rights and sought to address the consequences of displacement, yet the implementation of these resolutions has faced numerous challenges, including political roadblocks and lack of enforcement. The International Criminal Court (ICC) has also played a part in investigating potential war crimes and seeking accountability, but its efforts have often been met with resistance from powerful actors, limiting its impact on the ground. This section examines the successes and limitations of international law in holding parties accountable and in promoting justice for displaced populations.

Finally, the chapter explores potential avenues for reconciliation and accountability, looking beyond state-level actions to grassroots movements and civil society initiatives. Grassroots efforts, often led by Palestinians and Israelis who seek peace and justice, offer alternative pathways to reconciliation through dialogue, collaboration, and a shared commitment to acknowledging past wrongs. These initiatives are crucial in laying the groundwork for meaningful reconciliation and creating frameworks that foster coexistence. By understanding these different aspects of reparations and accountability, this chapter provides a comprehensive view of the challenges and possibilities for addressing historical injustices in Israel and Palestine, emphasizing the importance of recognition, restitution, and reconciliation in moving toward a more just future.

# Colonial Responsibility: Acknowledging Historical Injustices

**THE ETHICAL DEBATE Around Colonial Responsibility**

The question of colonial responsibility is at the heart of the debate over the Israeli-Palestinian conflict, as Israel's creation and subsequent expansion are often viewed through the lens of colonialism and the dispossession of an indigenous population. Acknowledging historical injustices is a complex and sensitive issue that involves ethical considerations about accountability, reparations, and the long-term impacts of colonial actions. In the case of Israel, the responsibility for historical injustices is intertwined with the broader context of European colonialism, Western intervention in the Middle East, and the legacy of European anti-Semitism that culminated in the Holocaust.

One key aspect of the ethical debate around colonial responsibility is whether modern states and societies should be held accountable for actions taken by previous generations. Supporters of acknowledging colonial responsibility argue that the impact of historical injustices, such as displacement, dispossession, and systemic discrimination, continues to affect marginalized populations today. In the context of Israel and Palestine, the displacement of Palestinians during the 1948 Nakba and subsequent conflicts has left millions of people as refugees, unable to return to their homes and living in conditions of statelessness and economic hardship. The ongoing impact of these events makes it imperative to address historical wrongs and seek avenues for reparative justice.

On the other hand, opponents of acknowledging colonial responsibility argue that contemporary generations cannot be held responsible for the actions of their ancestors and that focusing on historical grievances may hinder efforts to move forward and achieve reconciliation. In the case of Israel, some argue that the state's creation was a necessary response to the persecution of Jews in Europe and that holding Israel responsible for colonial-style actions ignores the context of Jewish suffering and the need for a secure homeland. This perspective suggests that the focus should be on finding a practical solution to the conflict rather than dwelling on past injustices.

The ethical debate also extends to the role of Western powers, particularly European countries and the United States, in the establishment of Israel and their continued support for its actions. The Balfour Declaration of 1917, in which Britain expressed support for the establishment of a "national home for the Jewish people" in Palestine, is often cited as an example of colonial interference that disregarded the rights and aspirations of the indigenous Arab population. Acknowledging this historical role requires Western powers to recognize their responsibility in shaping the conflict and to consider what steps they can take to address the consequences of their actions, including supporting a just resolution for Palestinian refugees and advocating for equal rights for all people living in the region.

**Comparisons with Other Post-Colonial Reparations Efforts**

The issue of colonial responsibility is not unique to Israel and Palestine, and comparisons can be drawn with other post-colonial reparations efforts around the world. In recent years, there has been a growing movement to acknowledge and address the injustices of colonialism, with several countries taking steps to provide reparations or at least formally apologize for their actions during the colonial era.

One notable example is Germany's efforts to address its colonial past in Namibia. In the early 20th century, German colonial forces carried out a genocide against the Herero and Nama people, resulting in the deaths of tens of thousands. In recent years, Germany has acknowledged this atrocity and has taken steps to provide reparations, including financial compensation and development aid to the affected communities. While the reparations have been criticized by some as insufficient, Germany's acknowledgment of its colonial responsibility represents an important step toward addressing historical injustices and promoting reconciliation.

Another example is the case of the British colonial government in Kenya, where thousands of Kenyans were subjected to torture and abuse during the Mau Mau uprising in the 1950s. In 2013, the British government formally apologized for the abuses and agreed to pay compensation to the surviving victims. This acknowledgment of responsibility, along with the financial reparations, was seen as a significant step in addressing the legacy of colonialism and recognizing the suffering of those who had been oppressed under British rule.

These examples highlight the potential for reparative justice to play a role in addressing historical wrongs and fostering reconciliation. In the context of Israel and Palestine, similar efforts could involve acknowledging the displacement of Palestinians during the creation of the state of Israel and providing compensation or support for refugees. This could take the form of financial compensation, the right of return for some refugees, or other measures aimed at addressing the ongoing impact of historical injustices. Such efforts would require a willingness on the part of Israel and its allies to confront difficult aspects of the past and to work toward a solution that acknowledges the rights and aspirations of both Israelis and Palestinians.

However, the comparison with other post-colonial contexts also underscores the challenges of pursuing reparative justice. In many cases, efforts to address historical injustices have been met with resistance, both from the governments responsible and from segments of the population who fear that acknowledging past wrongs could undermine national identity or lead to demands for significant concessions. In the case of Israel, the narrative of the state's creation as a necessary refuge for Jews following centuries of persecution is deeply ingrained in the national consciousness, making it difficult for many Israelis to view the displacement of Palestinians as a colonial injustice that requires redress.

Despite these challenges, the examples of other post-colonial reparations efforts demonstrate that acknowledging historical injustices is possible and can contribute to reconciliation and healing. Addressing the colonial dimensions of the Israeli-Palestinian conflict and taking steps toward reparative justice could help to create a foundation for a more just and lasting peace. This would require both sides, as well as the broader international community, to confront the complexities of history and to recognize the rights and humanity of all those affected by the conflict.

# Addressing Palestinian Displacement: Calls for Reparative Justice

## RIGHT OF RETURN: HISTORICAL and Legal Context

The right of return for Palestinian refugees is one of the most contentious issues in the Israeli-Palestinian conflict. It revolves around the displacement of hundreds of thousands of Palestinians during the 1948 Arab-Israeli War, known as the Nakba, and subsequent conflicts. During the Nakba, an estimated 750,000 Palestinians were either expelled from or fled their homes due to the violence and uncertainty that followed the establishment of the state of Israel. These refugees and their descendants, who now number in the millions, have since lived in refugee camps across the Middle East, often in dire conditions, with their right to return to their ancestral homes remaining unfulfilled.

The right of return is rooted in international law and has been enshrined in several United Nations resolutions. The most notable is UN General Assembly Resolution 194, passed in 1948, which explicitly states that refugees wishing to return to their homes should be permitted to do so and that compensation should be paid for those choosing not to return. This resolution forms the legal basis for Palestinian claims to the right of return and has been reaffirmed multiple times by the UN over the decades. For Palestinians, the right of return is not only a matter of international law but also a fundamental issue of justice, identity, and recognition of the suffering they have endured since their displacement.

For Israel, the right of return is a highly sensitive issue, as the return of millions of Palestinian refugees could potentially alter the demographic balance of the state, threatening its identity as a Jewish homeland. Israeli leaders have consistently opposed the idea of a mass return of Palestinian refugees, arguing that it would undermine the Jewish character of the state and that any solution to the refugee problem should involve resettlement in a future Palestinian state or compensation rather than repatriation. This stance has been a major obstacle in peace negotiations, with the right of return remaining a deeply divisive issue between the two sides.

Despite the challenges, calls for reparative justice for Palestinian refugees, including recognition of their right of return, remain central to any potential resolution of the conflict. The demand for the right of return is not simply about the physical return of refugees but also about acknowledging the historical injustice that was done to them and providing a sense of dignity and closure. For many Palestinians, the right of return symbolizes their connection to the land and their resilience in the face of decades of displacement and marginalization. Addressing this issue in a fair and just manner is crucial for achieving lasting peace and reconciliation between Israelis and Palestinians.

**Property Restitution and Compensation Efforts**

Another key aspect of addressing Palestinian displacement is the question of property restitution and compensation for those who were forced to leave their homes in 1948 and subsequent conflicts. During the Nakba, countless Palestinian homes, farms, and businesses were abandoned or seized by Jewish forces, and much of this property was subsequently transferred to the Israeli state or new Jewish immigrants. The loss of property has had a profound impact on Palestinian refugees, many of whom have lived in poverty and without basic rights for generations, unable to reclaim what they lost.

The issue of property restitution is inherently linked to the right of return. For those who wish to return to their ancestral homes, the question of whether they will be able to reclaim their property is a major concern. However, the practical challenges of restitution are significant, as much of the land and property once owned by Palestinians has since been developed or resettled by Jewish Israelis. The passage of time has made it difficult to determine rightful ownership, and many properties have changed hands multiple times, complicating the possibility of direct restitution. Nonetheless, for many Palestinian refugees, the recognition of their right to reclaim their property remains a powerful symbol of justice and acknowledgment of the wrongs they have suffered.

In addition to property restitution, compensation is often proposed as an alternative for those who do not wish to return or where restitution is not feasible. Compensation could take the form of financial payments for lost property, as well as compensation for the suffering and hardship endured by refugees over the decades. The idea of compensation has been included in various peace proposals, including the 2000 Camp David Summit and the Arab Peace Initiative of 2002, but no concrete mechanism for implementing such compensation has been established.

The role of the international community is crucial in any effort to address property restitution and compensation for Palestinian refugees. Given the financial and logistical challenges involved, international donors would likely need to play a significant role in funding compensation efforts, as well as in facilitating negotiations between Israel and the Palestinian leadership. Establishing an international commission to assess claims and determine compensation amounts has been suggested as a potential way forward, but such efforts would require the political will of all parties involved.

Addressing the issue of Palestinian displacement through property restitution and compensation is essential for achieving a just and lasting resolution to the conflict. Recognizing the losses suffered by Palestinian refugees and providing them with a sense of justice is not only a matter of legal obligation but also a moral imperative. The displacement of Palestinians is a central grievance that continues to fuel resentment and undermine prospects for peace. By addressing this issue in a fair and comprehensive manner, both sides can take a significant step toward reconciliation and the establishment of a lasting and just peace in the region.

# The Role of International Law and Global Organizations

**UNITED NATIONS RESOLUTIONS and Their Implementation Challenges**

The United Nations has played a prominent role in attempting to address the Israeli-Palestinian conflict, passing numerous resolutions that call for an end to hostilities, respect for human rights, and a peaceful resolution based on the principles of international law. Among the most notable UN resolutions are those that address the rights of Palestinian refugees, the status of Jerusalem, and the illegality of Israeli settlements in the occupied territories.

UN General Assembly Resolution 194, adopted in 1948, called for the return of Palestinian refugees wishing to live in peace with their neighbors and compensation for those who chose not to return. This resolution forms the basis for the Palestinian demand for the right of return, which remains a key issue in peace negotiations. Similarly, UN Security Council Resolution 242, adopted after the Six-Day War in 1967, calls for the withdrawal of Israeli forces from territories occupied during the conflict and emphasizes the need for a just solution to the refugee problem. Resolution 242 has served as a cornerstone for the "land for peace" formula in subsequent peace negotiations, including the Oslo Accords.

Despite these resolutions, their implementation has faced significant challenges. One of the primary obstacles is the lack of enforcement mechanisms within the UN system. Unlike domestic law, international law relies on the cooperation and goodwill of member states for enforcement, and there is no global authority with the power to compel states to comply. In the case of Israel and Palestine, the UN's ability to implement its resolutions has been hindered by political considerations, particularly the use of the veto power by the United

States in the Security Council. The United States has repeatedly blocked resolutions critical of Israel, effectively shielding it from international pressure and preventing the implementation of measures aimed at addressing the grievances of the Palestinian people.

Another challenge is the asymmetry of power between Israel and the Palestinians, which has made it difficult to achieve meaningful progress on the ground. While the UN has passed numerous resolutions calling for an end to settlement expansion, respect for human rights, and the establishment of a Palestinian state, Israel's superior military and economic power, combined with its strategic alliances with powerful countries, has allowed it to resist international pressure. The lack of consequences for non-compliance has further undermined the credibility of the UN and its ability to bring about a just resolution to the conflict.

The political divisions within the international community have also played a role in hindering the implementation of UN resolutions. While many countries support the Palestinian cause and advocate for the implementation of resolutions calling for an end to the occupation, others, particularly Western countries, have prioritized their strategic alliances with Israel. This division has made it difficult to build the consensus needed to take effective action, and the resulting paralysis has left the situation unresolved for decades.

**The Role of the International Criminal Court (ICC)**

The International Criminal Court (ICC) has emerged as another potential avenue for addressing the issue of accountability in the Israeli-Palestinian conflict. The ICC, established in 2002, is the first permanent international court with the mandate to prosecute individuals for war crimes, crimes against humanity, and genocide. The court's involvement in the Israeli-Palestinian conflict has been a contentious issue, with both sides accusing each other of committing war crimes and seeking to hold their opponents accountable.

In 2015, the Palestinian Authority (PA) became a party to the Rome Statute, the treaty that established the ICC, allowing the court to exercise jurisdiction over alleged crimes committed in the occupied Palestinian territories. In 2021, the ICC's chief prosecutor announced the opening of an investigation into alleged war crimes committed by both Israeli forces and Palestinian armed groups in the West Bank, Gaza Strip, and East Jerusalem. This investigation aims to address allegations of violations of international law, including the targeting of civilians, the use of disproportionate force, and the expansion of settlements in the occupied territories.

The involvement of the ICC has been met with strong opposition from Israel and its allies, particularly the United States. Israel, which is not a party to the Rome Statute, has argued that the ICC lacks jurisdiction over the matter, as it does not recognize Palestinian statehood. Israeli officials have also accused the court of bias and have refused to cooperate with the investigation. The United States has similarly opposed the investigation, arguing that it undermines efforts to resolve the conflict through negotiations and warning that it could have negative consequences for the peace process.

The challenges faced by the ICC in pursuing its investigation highlight the difficulties of applying international law in the context of the Israeli-Palestinian conflict. The lack of cooperation from Israel, combined with political pressure from powerful countries, has made it difficult for the court to carry out its mandate effectively. Moreover, the court's ability to enforce its decisions is limited, as it relies on the cooperation of member states to arrest suspects and carry out prosecutions. In the absence of such cooperation, the ICC's impact is largely symbolic, serving as a reminder of the principles of international law rather than a means of achieving accountability.

Despite these challenges, the ICC's involvement represents an important step toward addressing the issue of accountability in the Israeli-Palestinian conflict. The investigation has the potential to shed light on alleged violations of international law and to provide a measure of justice for the victims of the conflict. For Palestinians, the involvement of the ICC is seen as a way to address the power imbalance with Israel and to hold those responsible for alleged crimes accountable. For Israelis, however, the investigation is viewed as a threat to their sovereignty and security, and there are concerns that it could be used as a tool for political pressure.

The role of international law and global organizations in addressing the Israeli-Palestinian conflict is complex and fraught with challenges. While the United Nations and the ICC have the potential to play a significant role in promoting accountability and seeking a just resolution, their efforts have been hampered by political considerations, a lack of enforcement mechanisms, and the asymmetry of power between the parties. Nevertheless, the principles of international law remain an important reference point for those seeking justice and a peaceful resolution to the conflict, and the involvement of global organizations serves as a reminder of the need for accountability and respect for human rights.

# Potential Avenues for Reconciliation and Accountability

**GRASSROOTS MOVEMENTS and Civil Society Initiatives**

Grassroots movements and civil society initiatives play a crucial role in fostering reconciliation and promoting accountability in the Israeli-Palestinian conflict. Unlike governmental efforts, which are often influenced by political agendas and constraints, grassroots initiatives are driven by the desire of ordinary people on both sides to build bridges and find common ground. These initiatives aim to break down the barriers of hatred, mistrust, and prejudice that have accumulated over decades of conflict and to create spaces for dialogue, mutual understanding, and cooperation.

One of the most prominent grassroots movements is the Parents Circle – Families Forum, a joint Israeli-Palestinian organization made up of bereaved families who have lost loved ones in the conflict. The members of this group come together to share their stories of loss and to advocate for reconciliation and an end to violence. By focusing on the shared pain of loss, the Parents Circle aims to humanize the "other side" and challenge the narratives of hatred that perpetuate the conflict. The group organizes educational programs, public speaking events, and workshops that bring Israelis and Palestinians together, emphasizing the need for empathy and understanding as a basis for peace.

Another example of grassroots initiatives is Combatants for Peace, an organization founded by former Israeli soldiers and Palestinian fighters who have renounced violence and chosen to work together for a peaceful resolution to the conflict. Combatants for Peace engages in nonviolent protests, educational activities, and joint community projects that demonstrate the power of cooperation and dialogue. By highlighting the shared desire for peace among individuals who were once adversaries, the movement seeks to inspire others to reject violence and work toward reconciliation.

Civil society initiatives also include projects that focus on economic cooperation, environmental sustainability, and cultural exchange. Organizations such as EcoPeace Middle East bring together Israelis, Palestinians, and Jordanians to address shared environmental challenges, such as water scarcity and pollution. By working together on practical issues that affect everyone's lives, these initiatives create opportunities for collaboration and build trust between communities. Economic cooperation projects, such as joint business ventures and employment initiatives, aim to create economic interdependence and provide tangible benefits to both sides, fostering a sense of shared interest in peace and stability.

These grassroots movements and civil society initiatives face significant challenges, including opposition from hardliners on both sides, restrictions on movement, and limited funding. However, they represent a vital component of any effort to achieve reconciliation and accountability. By creating spaces for dialogue, challenging negative stereotypes, and promoting cooperation, these initiatives contribute to building the foundations for a future in which Israelis and Palestinians can coexist peacefully.

### Dialogue and Reconciliation Frameworks

Dialogue and reconciliation frameworks are essential for addressing the deep-rooted grievances and mistrust that have fueled the Israeli-Palestinian conflict for decades. These frameworks aim to create structured processes through which both sides can acknowledge past wrongs, address historical injustices, and work toward a shared vision of a peaceful future. Reconciliation is not only about achieving a political settlement but also about healing the wounds of conflict and creating the conditions for lasting peace.

One approach to dialogue and reconciliation is the concept of "truth and reconciliation" commissions, modeled after similar efforts in other post-conflict settings, such as South Africa and Rwanda. A truth and reconciliation commission for Israel and Palestine could provide a platform for individuals from both sides to share their experiences of the conflict, acknowledge the suffering of others, and seek forgiveness. Such a process would require the participation of both Israeli and Palestinian leaders, as well as representatives from civil society, religious groups, and victims' organizations. By creating an official record of the events of the conflict and acknowledging the harm done to both sides, a truth and reconciliation commission could help to foster a sense of accountability and lay the groundwork for reconciliation.

Dialogue frameworks can also take the form of community-based dialogue groups, where Israelis and Palestinians come together to discuss their perspectives on the conflict and explore ways to work toward peace. These groups often focus on building personal relationships and fostering empathy, allowing participants to see the humanity of those on the other side. Dialogue initiatives, such as those organized by the organization Seeds of Peace, bring together young people from both sides to engage in open discussions, develop leadership skills, and build friendships that transcend national and cultural divides. By focusing on young people, these initiatives aim to create a new generation of leaders who are committed to peace and reconciliation.

Reconciliation frameworks must also address the issue of accountability for past actions. This includes acknowledging the displacement of Palestinian refugees, recognizing the impact of the occupation, and addressing the grievances of both sides. Mechanisms for accountability could involve international oversight, legal processes, and agreements on reparative justice. The role of international organizations, such as the United Nations and the International Criminal Court, could be instrumental in ensuring that violations of international law are addressed and that both sides are held accountable for their actions. Accountability is a key component of reconciliation, as it provides a sense of justice for victims and helps to prevent future abuses.

The success of dialogue and reconciliation frameworks depends on the willingness of both sides to engage in meaningful dialogue and to make the necessary compromises for peace. It also requires the support of the international community, which can provide resources, facilitation, and guarantees for the implementation of agreements. Reconciliation is a long and difficult process, but it is essential for creating a sustainable peace that goes beyond political agreements and addresses the underlying causes of the conflict.

Grassroots movements, civil society initiatives, and structured dialogue and reconciliation frameworks offer potential avenues for addressing the deep-seated issues that have fueled the Israeli-Palestinian conflict. By promoting empathy, cooperation, and accountability, these efforts can help to create the conditions for a just and lasting peace. While the challenges are significant, the determination of individuals and communities to work toward reconciliation provides hope for a future in which Israelis and Palestinians can live side by side in peace and security.

# Chapter 9: The Modern Impact of European Colonial Legacy

Chapter 9 examines the modern impact of the European colonial legacy on Israel, exploring how European cultural, political, and ideological influences continue to shape Israeli society and its relationships both within the region and on the global stage. From its founding, Israel has been profoundly influenced by European ideas and values, which have played a major role in the development of its institutions and national identity. This influence is particularly evident in the education system, where European curricula have shaped the way history, politics, and culture are taught. The emphasis on European cultural norms has also contributed to the Westernization of Israeli society, creating a cultural identity that aligns more closely with Europe and the West than with its Middle Eastern neighbors.

The European origins of modern Israel have also significantly shaped its current geopolitical dynamics. Israel maintains close ties with the European Union, benefiting from trade agreements, political partnerships, and cultural exchanges. These relationships have influenced Israel's position in the international community and have provided it with diplomatic leverage. European political ideologies and alliances have also played a role in shaping Israel's approach to regional diplomacy and peace initiatives, often favoring strategies that align with Western interests and perspectives.

Israel's relationship with its neighboring Middle Eastern countries remains complex, characterized by a history of conflicts and shifting alliances. Since its establishment, Israel has experienced a series of wars and hostilities with neighboring Arab states, but it has also engaged in peace treaties and normalization agreements, such as those with Egypt and Jordan. These relationships are influenced by both historical grievances and the ongoing impact of European colonial attitudes, which have affected the way Israel and its neighbors perceive each other. Current diplomatic relations are marked by both cooperation and tension, as regional dynamics evolve in response to changing alliances and interests.

The role of Western powers, particularly the United States and European nations, in sustaining Israel's colonial legacy cannot be overstated. Military alliances and the presence of Western military technology have bolstered Israel's security, ensuring its dominance in the region. Economic dependencies, including trade relations and financial aid, have further entrenched Israel's ties to the West, creating a framework in which Israel's position as a powerful state is maintained by external support. This ongoing influence has perpetuated the legacy of colonialism, shaping the way Israel interacts with both its own population and the broader region.

By exploring these themes, Chapter 9 provides insight into how the European colonial legacy continues to impact modern Israel, affecting its cultural identity, geopolitical relationships, and the broader dynamics of power in the Middle East. The chapter highlights the interconnectedness of historical influences and contemporary realities, showing how the legacy of colonialism continues to shape the region's political landscape and Israel's role within it.

# Ongoing Influence of European Culture and Political Ideology in Israel

## EDUCATION SYSTEMS AND the Influence of European Curricula

The Israeli education system has been significantly shaped by European cultural and political ideologies, which have influenced both the content of curricula and the broader educational philosophy of the state. From the establishment of Israel, the founders, many of whom were of European origin, sought to create an education system that would reflect the values and historical experiences of European Jewry, emphasizing Zionism, the Holocaust, and the return to the Jewish homeland. This focus led to an emphasis on European history and the experiences of Ashkenazi Jews, while largely marginalizing the narratives and contributions of Jews from Middle Eastern, North African, and other non-European backgrounds.

The influence of European curricula is evident in the subjects taught in Israeli schools. History classes, for example, often focus on European Jewish history, including the pogroms, the Holocaust, and the Zionist movement's roots in Europe. These subjects are presented as central to the formation of modern Jewish identity, while the histories of Mizrahi, Sephardic, and Ethiopian Jews are frequently sidelined or given less importance. This Eurocentric focus has led to a situation in which many young Israelis are well-versed in the experiences of European Jews but have limited knowledge of the rich cultural heritage of Jewish communities from the Middle East and North Africa.

The emphasis on European education is also reflected in the teaching of literature, philosophy, and civics, where European authors and thinkers are often prioritized over those from other cultural backgrounds. The works of European philosophers, such as Theodor Herzl and Moses Mendelssohn, are central to the curriculum, while the contributions of non-European Jewish thinkers are often overlooked. This has contributed to a perception that European culture is more sophisticated or valuable, reinforcing the cultural hierarchy that exists within Israeli society.

The impact of this Eurocentric approach to education extends beyond the classroom and has shaped broader societal attitudes toward cultural identity. By prioritizing the experiences and values of European Jews, the education system has contributed to the marginalization of non-European Jews and has reinforced the dominance of Ashkenazi culture within Israeli society. This has had a lasting impact on the self-perception of Mizrahi, Sephardic, and Ethiopian Jews, many of whom have struggled to have their cultural heritage recognized and valued within the national narrative.

**Cultural Identity and Westernization in Israeli Society**

The influence of European culture and political ideology has also played a significant role in shaping Israeli cultural identity and contributing to the process of Westernization. The founders of the state, many of whom were European immigrants, brought with them a vision of a modern, Western-oriented society that would serve as a beacon of progress and development in the Middle East. This vision was reflected in the institutions they established, the cultural norms they promoted, and the values they sought to instill in the population.

One of the key aspects of this Westernization has been the adoption of European cultural norms and practices, which have come to dominate many aspects of Israeli life. European languages, particularly Hebrew as revived by European Jewish linguists, have become the standard, while the languages of Jews from Arab and Muslim countries, such as Arabic and Ladino, have been marginalized. Western styles of dress, music, and art have also become the norm, often at the expense of traditional Mizrahi and Sephardic cultural expressions. This process of Westernization has led to a situation in which the cultural contributions of non-European Jews are often undervalued or seen as less "modern" or "civilized."

The influence of European culture is also evident in Israeli political ideology, which has been shaped by Western concepts of nationalism, democracy, and liberalism. The Zionist movement, which laid the foundation for the state of Israel, was deeply influenced by European nationalist movements of the 19th century, which emphasized the importance of a shared national identity, territorial sovereignty, and self-determination. These ideas were transplanted to the Middle East, where they formed the basis for the creation of a Jewish state. However, the application of European nationalist principles in a region with a diverse population has led to tensions and conflicts, particularly with the indigenous Palestinian population, whose own aspirations for self-determination have been in direct conflict with the Zionist project.

The Western orientation of Israeli society is also reflected in its close ties to the United States and Europe, both politically and culturally. Israel has long sought to align itself with Western powers, viewing itself as part of the Western world and seeking to distinguish itself from its Middle Eastern neighbors. This alignment has influenced Israeli foreign policy, economic development, and cultural exchanges, reinforcing the perception that Israel is a Western enclave in the Middle East. The strong cultural and political ties between Israel and Western countries have also contributed to the adoption of Western consumer culture, lifestyle, and values, which have become increasingly prevalent in Israeli society.

While the influence of European culture and Westernization has brought many benefits to Israel, including economic development, technological advancement, and strong international alliances, it has also created significant cultural tensions within the country. The dominance of European culture has marginalized the experiences and contributions of non-European Jews, leading to a sense of exclusion and alienation among these communities. Efforts to address these disparities, such as promoting the cultural heritage of Mizrahi and Sephardic Jews, have gained momentum in recent years, but the legacy of European influence remains a powerful force in shaping Israeli identity.

The ongoing influence of European culture and political ideology in Israel has had a profound impact on the country's education system, cultural identity, and societal values. While this influence has helped to shape Israel into a modern, Western-oriented state, it has also contributed to the marginalization of non-European Jews and the creation of a cultural hierarchy within Israeli society. Addressing these issues requires a more inclusive approach that recognizes and values the diverse cultural contributions of all Jewish communities and seeks to create a more balanced and representative national narrative.

# How European Origins Shape Current Geopolitical Dynamics

**RELATIONS WITH THE European Union**

Israel's European origins have significantly shaped its relationship with the European Union, both in terms of economic cooperation and political alignment. Many of Israel's founding leaders were influenced by European political thought, and this cultural connection has fostered strong ties with Europe over the decades. The EU is one of Israel's largest trading partners, and the relationship is underpinned by agreements that facilitate the exchange of goods, services, and technology. The EU-Israel Association Agreement, signed in 2000, forms the foundation of this partnership, allowing for preferential trade and cooperation in areas such as research, science, and technological innovation.

European nations and the EU as a whole have also provided significant funding and support to Israel's economic development, contributing to infrastructure projects, research initiatives, and technological advancements. Israel's participation in EU programs such as Horizon 2020 and its successor, Horizon Europe, has enabled collaboration between Israeli and European researchers, fostering innovation in fields like cybersecurity, medicine, and environmental technology. This cooperation reflects the shared values of progress and development that are rooted in Israel's European-influenced identity.

However, the relationship between Israel and the EU is complex, as it is not solely based on economic and scientific cooperation. The EU has been a vocal critic of certain Israeli policies, particularly regarding settlement expansion in the West Bank and the treatment of Palestinians. The European Union has consistently emphasized the need for a two-state solution and has called on Israel to halt settlement activities, which it views as illegal under international law. This stance has led to tensions between Israel and the EU, with Israeli leaders often accusing European countries of bias and undue interference in Israel's internal affairs.

The European origins of Israel have influenced the way the country is perceived by European nations, as well as the expectations placed upon it. Many European governments see Israel as a fellow democracy that shares their values of human rights, the rule of law, and political pluralism. This perception has led the EU to maintain a strong partnership with Israel despite disagreements on specific policies. At the same time, the cultural and political affinity between Israel and Europe has also led to frustration among European leaders when Israeli actions are perceived as conflicting with these shared values, particularly in the context of the Israeli-Palestinian conflict.

**Influence on Regional Diplomacy and Peace Initiatives**

Israel's European origins have also played a significant role in shaping its approach to regional diplomacy and its involvement in peace initiatives. From its founding, Israel has sought to position itself as a Western-oriented state in the Middle East, drawing on European political ideologies and diplomatic strategies to navigate its relationships with neighboring countries. This Western alignment has influenced Israel's foreign policy decisions, particularly in the context of alliances and peace negotiations.

The influence of European diplomatic traditions is evident in Israel's approach to peace initiatives with its Arab neighbors. The emphasis on bilateral negotiations, compromise, and incremental progress, which has characterized many of Israel's peace agreements, reflects a European diplomatic approach. This can be seen in the Israel-Egypt Peace Treaty of 1979 and the Israel-Jordan Peace Treaty of 1994, both of which involved extensive negotiations and the mediation of Western powers. The involvement of the United States, a key ally with strong European ties, has further reinforced this approach, as

American mediation has often been shaped by Western diplomatic principles.

Israel's European orientation has also influenced its relationship with non-Arab regional actors, such as Turkey and Iran. In the early decades of Israel's existence, it maintained close relations with Turkey, another Western-aligned state in the region. This relationship was characterized by economic cooperation, military collaboration, and a shared interest in countering Arab nationalism. However, as Turkey's foreign policy shifted under President Recep Tayyip Erdoğan, relations between the two countries have become strained, with Israel's Western alignment increasingly seen as a point of divergence.

The influence of European political ideology is also evident in Israel's efforts to build alliances with other Middle Eastern countries in recent years. The Abraham Accords, which normalized relations between Israel and several Arab states, including the United Arab Emirates and Bahrain, were driven by a pragmatic approach to regional diplomacy that draws on Western principles of economic cooperation and mutual security. These agreements reflect a shift in regional dynamics, as shared concerns over Iran and the desire for economic development have led to a reconfiguration of alliances, with Israel positioning itself as a partner to other states seeking modernization and stability.

At the same time, Israel's European roots have contributed to its challenges in fully integrating into the Middle East. Many Arab countries have long viewed Israel as an extension of Western colonial influence in the region, a perception that has been reinforced by Israel's close ties to European and American powers. This perception has made it difficult for Israel to gain acceptance among its neighbors and has fueled resistance to normalization efforts. The ongoing conflict with the Palestinians, and Israel's policies in the occupied territories, are also seen by many in the region as evidence of a colonial mindset that prioritizes control over indigenous rights.

The European origins of Israel have had a profound impact on its geopolitical dynamics, influencing both its relationships with Western powers and its approach to regional diplomacy. The cultural, political, and economic ties between Israel and Europe have fostered strong partnerships, but they have also contributed to tensions with neighboring countries that view Israel as an outsider in the region. As Israel continues to navigate its complex relationships in the Middle East, the legacy of its European origins will continue to shape its foreign policy and its efforts to achieve lasting peace and security.

# Israel's Relationship with Neighboring Middle Eastern Countries

## HISTORICAL CONFLICTS and Treaties

Israel's relationship with its neighboring Middle Eastern countries has been defined by a series of conflicts, wars, and subsequent peace treaties. From the moment of its establishment in 1948, Israel was thrust into conflict with its Arab neighbors, as the newly declared state faced military opposition from a coalition of Arab nations, including Egypt, Jordan, Syria, Lebanon, and Iraq. This conflict, known as the 1948 Arab-Israeli War, resulted in the armistice agreements of 1949, which established the borders of the state but left the underlying tensions unresolved.

The 1956 Suez Crisis was another significant moment in Israel's regional relationships, as it joined forces with France and the United Kingdom in a military campaign against Egypt following President Gamal Abdel Nasser's nationalization of the Suez Canal. Although Israel achieved military success, international pressure led to a withdrawal, and the incident further complicated Israel's relations with its neighbors.

The Six-Day War of 1967 marked a turning point in Israel's relationship with the region. In a preemptive strike against the amassed forces of Egypt, Syria, and Jordan, Israel captured the West Bank, Gaza Strip, Sinai Peninsula, and the Golan Heights. The war significantly altered the geopolitical landscape, with Israel tripling its territory and gaining control over key areas, including East Jerusalem. However, the occupation of these territories also led to increased tensions with the Palestinian population and the international community, as well as creating new fronts of conflict with neighboring states.

The 1973 Yom Kippur War, launched by Egypt and Syria in an attempt to regain territories lost in 1967, further strained Israel's relations with its neighbors. Although Israel was ultimately able to repel the attack, the war underscored the fragility of the regional balance of power and the ongoing hostility between Israel and its Arab neighbors.

Despite these conflicts, Israel has also taken significant steps toward peace with some of its neighbors. The 1979 Camp David Accords, brokered by the United States, led to a historic peace treaty between Israel and Egypt, making Egypt the first Arab country to officially recognize Israel. In return, Israel agreed to withdraw from the Sinai Peninsula, which it had occupied since 1967. The treaty marked a significant shift in the region, demonstrating the potential for diplomacy to overcome decades of hostility.

In 1994, Israel signed a peace treaty with Jordan, normalizing relations and establishing formal diplomatic ties. This treaty was facilitated by the progress made in the Oslo Accords between Israel and the Palestinian Liberation Organization (PLO), which created a more conducive environment for peace with Jordan. The Israel-Jordan peace treaty has since provided a framework for cooperation on issues such as water sharing, security, and economic development, although it has faced challenges due to ongoing tensions over the Israeli-Palestinian conflict.

**Current Diplomatic Relations and Tensions**

In recent years, Israel's relationships with its neighboring countries have evolved significantly, with a mix of diplomatic breakthroughs and ongoing tensions. The Abraham Accords, signed in 2020, marked a major shift in Israel's regional relations, as the United Arab Emirates (UAE), Bahrain, Sudan, and Morocco agreed to normalize ties with Israel. These agreements were driven by shared economic interests, technological cooperation, and a common concern over the growing influence of Iran in the region. The normalization of relations with these countries has opened up new opportunities for trade, tourism, and strategic partnerships, and has reshaped the regional diplomatic landscape.

The Abraham Accords also highlighted a broader shift in the priorities of some Arab states, which have moved away from the traditional stance of non-recognition of Israel until a resolution to the Palestinian issue is reached. Instead, these countries have prioritized their own national interests, including economic development and security cooperation, over the Palestinian cause. While the normalization agreements have been welcomed by Israel as a significant diplomatic achievement, they have been met with criticism from Palestinians, who view them as a betrayal of their struggle for statehood.

Despite these diplomatic gains, Israel's relationships with other neighboring countries, such as Lebanon and Syria, remain tense and fraught with conflict. The border with Lebanon is a particularly volatile area, largely due to the presence of Hezbollah, a militant group backed by Iran that is committed to Israel's destruction. The 2006 Lebanon War between Israel and Hezbollah was a major escalation of this tension, resulting in significant casualties and destruction on both sides. Since then, the border has remained relatively quiet but highly militarized, with frequent skirmishes and the risk of renewed conflict always present.

Israel's relationship with Syria is similarly marked by hostility, largely due to the Israeli occupation of the Golan Heights, which was captured during the Six-Day War and later annexed by Israel in 1981. The international community has not recognized this annexation, and Syria continues to demand the return of the Golan Heights. The ongoing civil war in Syria has further complicated the situation, with Israel conducting airstrikes against Iranian and Hezbollah targets in Syria to prevent the establishment of a permanent military presence by its adversaries.

The relationship between Israel and the Palestinians remains the most significant and complex issue affecting Israel's standing in the region. Despite attempts at peace negotiations, including the Oslo Accords of the 1990s and subsequent efforts, a final resolution to the conflict has yet to be achieved. The expansion of Israeli settlements in the West Bank, the blockade of Gaza, and the periodic outbreaks of violence have all contributed to the continued impasse. The lack of progress on the Palestinian issue remains a source of tension not only between Israel and the Palestinians but also with neighboring countries, including Jordan and Egypt, which have expressed concern over the potential for instability.

Israel's ongoing occupation of Palestinian territories and its policies toward the Palestinian population have also affected its broader regional relationships. While some Arab countries have chosen to normalize relations with Israel, others, such as Iraq and Algeria, remain firmly opposed to any engagement with Israel as long as the Palestinian issue remains unresolved. The broader Arab public sentiment also remains largely sympathetic to the Palestinian cause, and this has limited the extent to which Arab governments can engage with Israel without facing domestic backlash.

Overall, Israel's relationships with its neighboring Middle Eastern countries are characterized by a combination of diplomatic successes and unresolved conflicts. The peace treaties with Egypt and Jordan and the normalization agreements with several Arab states demonstrate the potential for diplomacy and cooperation, while the ongoing tensions with Lebanon, Syria, and the Palestinians highlight the challenges that remain. The evolving geopolitical dynamics in the region, including the shifting priorities of Arab states and the influence of external actors like Iran, will continue to shape Israel's relationships with its neighbors and the prospects for long-term peace and stability.

# The Role of Western Powers in Sustaining Israel's Colonial Legacy

## MILITARY PRESENCE AND Alliances

Western powers, particularly the United States, have played a crucial role in sustaining Israel's security and ensuring its military superiority in the region. This support has contributed to what some view as a continuation of a colonial legacy, as it has enabled Israel to maintain control over occupied Palestinian territories and resist international calls for withdrawal. The military presence and alliances forged between Israel and Western countries have ensured that Israel remains a dominant force in the Middle East, with the capacity to defend itself against any regional adversaries.

The United States has been Israel's most significant ally in terms of military support. Since the 1970s, the United States has provided Israel with billions of dollars in military aid, which has allowed it to build one of the most advanced armed forces in the world. The U.S. also provides Israel with access to advanced weaponry, including fighter jets, missile defense systems, and precision-guided munitions. This military assistance has ensured that Israel retains a qualitative military edge (QME) over its neighbors, enabling it to effectively deter threats and maintain its security.

In addition to direct military aid, the United States and Israel have engaged in joint military exercises, intelligence sharing, and defense technology collaboration. These activities have strengthened Israel's defense capabilities and reinforced the strategic partnership between the two nations. The U.S. military presence in the region, including bases in countries such as Qatar and Bahrain, has also served as a deterrent to potential threats against Israel, ensuring that the country remains secure in a volatile region.

The strategic alliances with Western powers have also extended to European countries, particularly during the early years of Israel's existence. France, for example, was a major military partner of Israel in the 1950s and 1960s, providing weapons and assisting in the development of Israel's nuclear program. Although the relationship between Israel and European countries has evolved over the years, military cooperation has continued, with European nations providing training, technology, and intelligence support to Israel.

These military alliances have had a significant impact on Israel's ability to maintain control over the occupied Palestinian territories. The continued expansion of settlements in the West Bank, the blockade of Gaza, and military operations in Palestinian areas have all been made possible, in part, by the military support provided by Western powers. This support has enabled Israel to pursue policies that are widely seen as violating international law, including the construction of settlements on occupied land and the use of force against civilian populations. The military backing of Western countries has thus played a central role in sustaining Israel's presence in the occupied territories and reinforcing its control over the Palestinian population.

**Economic Dependencies and Trade Relations**

The economic relationship between Israel and Western powers has also played a significant role in sustaining Israel's colonial legacy. The economic support provided by the United States and European countries has been instrumental in the development of Israel's economy, allowing it to become one of the most advanced economies in the Middle East. This economic dependency has ensured that Israel remains closely aligned with Western interests and that it continues to benefit from the financial and technological support of its allies.

The United States provides Israel with significant economic aid, in addition to its military assistance. This aid has been used to support infrastructure projects, social services, and economic development initiatives, which have contributed to Israel's economic growth and stability. The close economic ties between the two countries are further reinforced by trade relations, with the United States being one of Israel's largest trading partners. The Free Trade Agreement between the U.S. and Israel, signed in 1985, was the first such agreement the United States entered into and has facilitated the growth of bilateral trade, particularly in high-tech goods and services.

European countries also play a significant role in Israel's economy. The European Union is Israel's largest trading partner, with extensive trade in goods, services, and technology. The EU-Israel Association Agreement, which grants Israel preferential access to European markets, has been a key factor in the growth of Israel's export-oriented economy. Israel's participation in EU research and development programs has further strengthened economic ties, allowing for collaboration in fields such as technology, medicine, and agriculture. These economic relations have provided Israel with access to the financial resources and markets necessary for its continued growth and development.

The economic support and trade relations with Western powers have also played a role in sustaining Israel's presence in the occupied territories. The growth of settlements in the West Bank, for example, has been facilitated by economic investments and infrastructure development, which have been supported by both public and private actors in Western countries. The export of settlement products to European and American markets has provided financial support for the expansion of these settlements, despite international calls for a boycott of goods produced in the occupied territories.

Western economic support has also contributed to the development of Israel's high-tech sector, which has been a major driver of the country's economic growth. The defense and technology industries, in particular, have benefited from collaboration with Western countries, allowing Israel to develop advanced military technologies that have been used in the occupied territories. The economic dependency on Western markets and the close integration of Israel's economy with those of Western countries have thus played a role in sustaining the policies that many view as part of a colonial legacy.

The role of Western powers in sustaining Israel's colonial legacy cannot be overstated. The military and economic support provided by the United States and European countries has enabled Israel to maintain its control over the occupied Palestinian territories and resist international calls for withdrawal. The strategic alliances and economic dependencies that have developed between Israel and the West have ensured that Israel remains a powerful and economically advanced state, capable of pursuing policies that are widely viewed as colonial in nature. Addressing these issues will require a reexamination of the role of Western powers in the conflict and a commitment to promoting a just and lasting resolution that respects the rights of all people in the region.

# Chapter 10: Israel in the Context of Global Colonialism

Chapter 10 places Israel within the broader context of global colonialism, examining its similarities and differences with other colonial ventures led by European powers. Throughout history, European colonialism has taken many forms, from settler colonies like Algeria and South Africa to the economic and administrative colonial rule seen in India. By comparing Israel to these case studies, the chapter highlights the shared characteristics of displacement, land appropriation, and cultural imposition that define many colonial endeavors, while also acknowledging the unique aspects of the Zionist project and its historical context. This comparison sheds light on how Israel's foundation was influenced by colonial strategies and ideologies, yet also diverged in certain ways that reflect the distinct nature of its establishment.

The experiences of other colonies that have undergone decolonization provide important lessons for the Israeli-Palestinian context. Decolonization movements, from India's struggle for independence to South Africa's transition from apartheid, offer valuable insights into strategies for achieving independence, fostering reconciliation, and addressing historical injustices. These examples underscore the importance of dialogue, resistance, and international pressure in challenging colonial structures. The chapter explores how these lessons could be applied to the Palestinian struggle for self-determination and what a potential path toward reconciliation might look like in the Israeli-Palestinian conflict.

In the 21st century, Israel stands as one of the last vestiges of a colonial project in an increasingly decolonized world. The persistence of this colonial legacy raises questions about the future of Israel's identity and its relationships with both regional and global powers. The ongoing global colonial dynamics, including neo-colonial practices and power imbalances, continue to shape the ways in which Israel interacts with the world. This section considers the evolving role of Israel and whether its colonial heritage will continue to define its place on the international stage or if there is potential for transformation.

The chapter also addresses the future of colonial dynamics in the Middle East, examining how shifting power structures are reshaping the region. Regional powers, such as Turkey, Iran, and Saudi Arabia, are increasingly asserting their influence, challenging the traditional dominance of Western-backed Israel. These shifts may offer opportunities for addressing historical legacies and reshaping relationships in the region. By placing Israel in the context of global colonialism, the chapter provides a broader perspective on the forces that have shaped its past and continue to influence its present and future, highlighting both the challenges and the possibilities for change in an evolving geopolitical landscape.

# Comparing Israel with Other European Colonial Ventures

## CASE STUDIES: ALGERIA, South Africa, and India

Israel's establishment and its ongoing control over Palestinian territories have drawn comparisons to other European colonial ventures, including the French colonization of Algeria, the British colonization of India, and the apartheid regime in South Africa. Examining these historical cases provides insight into the nature of Israel's policies and practices, as well as the broader dynamics of settler colonialism and resistance.

The French colonization of Algeria, which began in 1830, involved the settlement of hundreds of thousands of French citizens, known as "colons" or "pieds-noirs," who came to dominate the political, economic, and social life of the country. The indigenous Algerian population faced significant discrimination and exclusion, as well as expropriation of their land to benefit European settlers. The settlers enjoyed privileges that were denied to the indigenous population, who were treated as second-class citizens in their own land. This system of domination and exclusion led to a powerful anti-colonial movement, culminating in the Algerian War of Independence (1954-1962), during which the Algerian people fought against French colonial rule. The parallels with Israel are evident in the way land has been expropriated from Palestinians to benefit Jewish settlers, the establishment of settlements that serve to entrench Israeli control, and the ongoing resistance of the Palestinian people to these policies.

The case of South Africa, particularly under the apartheid regime, has also been frequently compared to Israel's treatment of Palestinians. Apartheid South Africa was characterized by a system of racial segregation and discrimination, in which the white minority population held political and economic power over the Black majority.

The apartheid government established separate territories known as "Bantustans," where Black South Africans were forced to live, while whites controlled the most fertile land and resources. This system of segregation has been likened to Israel's policies in the West Bank, where Palestinians are restricted to certain areas while Jewish settlers control large swathes of territory. The construction of the separation barrier, the network of checkpoints, and the restrictions on Palestinian movement have all drawn comparisons to the apartheid system, leading many to describe the situation in the occupied territories as a form of apartheid.

The British colonization of India offers another point of comparison. The British East India Company initially established control over Indian territories through trade and strategic alliances, before eventually expanding its influence to direct colonial rule. The British exploited India's resources for their own benefit, imposed heavy taxes on the local population, and implemented policies that led to widespread poverty and famine. The Indian independence movement, led by figures such as Mahatma Gandhi, was characterized by both nonviolent resistance and armed struggle against British rule. The situation in Israel and Palestine shares similarities with the British colonial project in India, particularly in terms of the economic exploitation of occupied territories and the imposition of policies that benefit the colonizers at the expense of the indigenous population. The resistance movements in Palestine, including both armed groups and nonviolent activists, also bear similarities to the struggle for independence in India.

### Similarities and Differences in Colonial Practices

There are several similarities between Israel's practices in the occupied Palestinian territories and those of other European colonial ventures. One key similarity is the use of settlements to establish control over the land. In Algeria, South Africa, and Israel, settlers were encouraged to move into the colonized territory, often with the support of the state, to establish a permanent presence that would solidify the colonizer's control. In Israel, the establishment of settlements in the West Bank has been a central feature of its colonial strategy, with settlers receiving government incentives such as housing subsidies, infrastructure development, and military protection. This practice mirrors the French and British colonial strategies of settling their own populations in the colonized lands to assert dominance and control.

Another similarity is the use of legal frameworks to legitimize the dispossession of the indigenous population. In Algeria, the French authorities implemented laws that allowed for the expropriation of land from the indigenous population to benefit the settlers. In South Africa, apartheid laws institutionalized racial segregation and ensured that the white minority retained control over the land and resources. Similarly, Israel has used a combination of military orders, legal mechanisms, and bureaucratic procedures to expropriate Palestinian land, restrict building permits, and establish settlements. These legal frameworks have served to entrench Israeli control over the occupied territories while denying Palestinians the ability to assert their rights.

There are also notable differences between Israel's colonial practices and those of other European colonial ventures. One key difference is the ideological basis for colonization. In Algeria, South Africa, and India, colonization was driven primarily by economic interests and the desire for territorial expansion. The settlers sought to exploit the natural resources of the colonized land and establish economic dominance. In contrast, the Zionist movement, which led to the establishment of Israel, was driven by a combination of religious, historical, and nationalist motivations. The desire to create a homeland for the Jewish people, particularly in the aftermath of centuries of persecution culminating in the Holocaust, was a central motivation for the establishment of Israel. This ideological basis has been used to justify the colonization of Palestinian territories, with Zionist leaders framing the settlement of the land as a fulfillment of a historical and religious right.

Another difference is the level of international support for the colonial project. While the colonization of Algeria, South Africa, and India eventually faced widespread international condemnation, Israel has received significant support from Western powers, particularly the United States and several European countries. This support has allowed Israel to continue its policies in the occupied territories without facing the same level of international pressure or isolation that other colonial powers experienced. The influence of the Jewish diaspora, particularly in Western countries, has also played a role in shaping international attitudes toward Israel and its policies.

A further difference lies in the response of the indigenous population. In Algeria and India, the anti-colonial movements eventually succeeded in driving out the colonizers and achieving independence. In South Africa, the apartheid regime was dismantled through a combination of internal resistance and international pressure, leading to the establishment of a democratic government. In the case of Israel and Palestine, however, a resolution to the conflict has yet to be achieved, and the Palestinian territories remain under Israeli occupation. The ongoing nature of the conflict, as well as the asymmetry of power between Israel and the Palestinians, has made it difficult for the Palestinian people to achieve their aspirations for independence and self-determination.

Comparing Israel's practices with those of other European colonial ventures provides important insights into the nature of the Israeli-Palestinian conflict and the challenges involved in achieving a just resolution. The similarities in terms of settlement, legal frameworks, and the treatment of the indigenous population suggest that Israel's policies in the occupied territories are consistent with those of other colonial projects. At the same time, the unique ideological motivations behind the establishment of Israel and the level of international support it has received highlight the complexities of the situation and the need for a nuanced approach to resolving the conflict. Addressing the colonial dimensions of Israel's policies is essential for understanding the grievances of the Palestinian people and working toward a solution that respects the rights and dignity of all those involved.

# Lessons from Other Decolonization Movements

**STRATEGIES FOR INDEPENDENCE and Reconciliation**

Decolonization movements across the world have provided valuable lessons in the pursuit of independence and reconciliation for colonized populations. By examining successful decolonization efforts, such as those in India, Algeria, and South Africa, one can gain insights into the strategies that helped achieve freedom from colonial rule and the processes that facilitated reconciliation between former colonizers and colonized.

In India, the independence movement was characterized by a combination of mass mobilization, nonviolent resistance, and the leadership of key figures such as Mahatma Gandhi and Jawaharlal Nehru. Gandhi's philosophy of nonviolent resistance, or "Satyagraha," became a powerful tool for galvanizing the Indian population against British colonial rule. This strategy emphasized the moral high ground and aimed to win international sympathy for the Indian cause. The use of peaceful protests, boycotts, and civil disobedience demonstrated the power of nonviolent struggle in achieving political change, even against a powerful colonial authority. The Indian movement's ability to unite diverse religious, linguistic, and cultural groups under a common cause also contributed to its success, highlighting the importance of national unity in the fight for independence.

The Algerian War of Independence, in contrast, was characterized by armed struggle and guerrilla warfare. Led by the National Liberation Front (FLN), Algerians waged a brutal war against French colonial forces, employing tactics that included both rural guerrilla campaigns and urban warfare. The FLN's ability to mobilize the population, gain support from neighboring countries, and garner international sympathy for their struggle played a crucial role in their eventual success. The Algerian experience demonstrates that armed resistance can be an effective strategy in achieving independence when the colonized population is able to sustain a prolonged struggle and build international alliances. The role of regional support, particularly from neighboring Arab countries, was crucial in providing refuge and resources to Algerian fighters, highlighting the importance of regional solidarity in anti-colonial movements.

South Africa's decolonization movement provides a different perspective, emphasizing the importance of negotiation, reconciliation, and the role of international pressure. The apartheid regime was dismantled through a combination of internal resistance, led by figures such as Nelson Mandela and organizations like the African National Congress (ANC), and international pressure in the form of sanctions, divestment campaigns, and diplomatic isolation. The willingness of the apartheid government to engage in negotiations with the ANC, along with Mandela's emphasis on reconciliation rather than revenge, allowed for a peaceful transition to a democratic government. The establishment of the Truth and Reconciliation Commission (TRC) after the end of apartheid provided a platform for victims and perpetrators to share their stories, acknowledge past wrongs, and seek forgiveness. The South African experience highlights the importance of dialogue, negotiation, and a commitment to reconciliation in overcoming the legacy of colonialism and building a more inclusive society.

### The Potential Path for Palestine

The lessons from these decolonization movements can provide guidance for the Palestinian struggle for independence and self-determination. While each historical context is unique, there are several strategies that Palestinians could adopt to further their cause, drawing inspiration from the successes and challenges faced by other movements.

One potential path for Palestine is the emphasis on nonviolent resistance and international solidarity, similar to the Indian independence movement. Palestinians have already engaged in various forms of nonviolent protest, such as demonstrations, boycotts, and international campaigns like the Boycott, Divestment, Sanctions (BDS) movement. The BDS movement, in particular, aims to apply economic and political pressure on Israel to end its occupation of Palestinian territories and recognize the rights of Palestinian refugees. By emphasizing nonviolent resistance and appealing to the international community for support, Palestinians can build global solidarity and challenge Israel's policies in a way that highlights the moral legitimacy of their struggle.

Another potential strategy is to build regional alliances and seek support from neighboring countries, as was done by the Algerian independence movement. The support of Arab countries has been an important factor in the Palestinian struggle, providing political backing, financial assistance, and a platform for raising awareness of the Palestinian cause. Strengthening these regional alliances and fostering unity among Arab states in support of Palestinian rights could help create the conditions necessary for achieving independence. However, this approach also faces challenges, as the normalization of relations between some Arab states and Israel in recent years has shifted regional dynamics and reduced the level of unified support for the Palestinian cause.

The South African model of negotiation and reconciliation also offers valuable lessons for Palestine. While armed resistance has been a part of the Palestinian struggle, the experience of South Africa suggests that a negotiated settlement, combined with a commitment to reconciliation, may offer a more viable path to achieving a lasting peace. Engaging in dialogue with Israeli leaders and working toward a two-state solution or a shared political framework that guarantees equal rights for all inhabitants of the region could help to break the cycle of violence and build a foundation for coexistence. The establishment of a truth and reconciliation process, in which both sides acknowledge past wrongs and seek to address grievances, could also play a role in healing the wounds of the conflict and fostering a more inclusive future.

The role of international pressure is another critical factor in the Palestinian struggle. Just as international sanctions and divestment campaigns played a role in dismantling apartheid in South Africa, international pressure on Israel could help create the conditions for a just resolution to the conflict. Building alliances with countries, civil society organizations, and movements around the world that support Palestinian rights can help to amplify the call for justice and accountability. The success of such efforts will depend on the ability of Palestinian leaders to effectively communicate their cause and build broad-based support that transcends political and cultural boundaries.

Ultimately, the path to independence and reconciliation for Palestine will require a combination of strategies, drawing on the lessons of other decolonization movements while adapting to the unique challenges of the Israeli-Palestinian conflict. Nonviolent resistance, regional alliances, negotiation, and international pressure all have a role to play in achieving the goal of self-determination and justice for the Palestinian people. The struggle for Palestine is not only about achieving political independence but also about addressing the historical injustices that have been inflicted upon the Palestinian population and creating a future in which all people in the region can live in peace, dignity, and equality.

# The Last Vestige of Colonialism: Israel's Place in the 21st Century

## ONGOING GLOBAL COLONIAL Dynamics

In the 21st century, the legacy of colonialism continues to influence global dynamics, and Israel's ongoing control over Palestinian territories is often viewed as a continuation of the colonial paradigm. While traditional colonial empires have largely dissolved, the remnants of their influence persist in the form of economic dependencies, territorial disputes, and geopolitical power imbalances. Israel's situation in the Middle East, with its established settlements in occupied territories, separation barriers, and military control over the West Bank and Gaza, is seen by many as the last vestige of a colonial mindset that seeks to dominate an indigenous population.

The dynamics of global power and support from Western nations have allowed Israel to maintain its control over Palestinian territories despite international criticism. Unlike other former colonial powers that were pressured to relinquish control over their colonies, Israel has received significant political, military, and economic backing, particularly from the United States and European countries, which has enabled it to continue its policies without facing significant consequences. This support has allowed Israel to defy numerous United Nations resolutions calling for an end to the occupation and the recognition of Palestinian rights.

The broader context of global colonial dynamics also includes the way in which powerful countries continue to influence weaker nations through indirect control and economic dependency. In many ways, Israel's relationship with the Palestinian territories reflects this pattern, where economic and military dominance is used to maintain control over a marginalized population. The dependency of the Palestinian economy on Israel, restrictions on movement, and control over resources such as water and land are all manifestations of a colonial-style relationship that continues to shape the daily lives of Palestinians. The situation exemplifies how colonial practices can persist in new forms, even in an era where formal colonial rule is largely considered a relic of the past.

Israel's relationship with its Arab neighbors is also influenced by the ongoing legacy of colonialism. Many in the region view Israel as an extension of Western colonial influence, particularly given the historical role of European powers in facilitating the establishment of the state. The normalization of relations with several Arab countries through the Abraham Accords has shifted regional dynamics, but it has not fundamentally addressed the perception of Israel as a colonial entity. Instead, it has highlighted the ways in which power, influence, and alliances continue to shape the region in ways that reflect the legacies of colonial-era geopolitics.

**The Future of Israel and Its Colonial Heritage**

The question of whether Israel can move beyond its colonial heritage and establish a new relationship with the Palestinian people is central to determining its future place in the 21st century. The continued expansion of settlements in the West Bank and the policies that restrict Palestinian rights have reinforced the perception of Israel as a colonial power, and addressing this perception will require significant changes in both policy and mindset.

One possible path forward is the pursuit of a two-state solution, which has long been seen as the most viable way to resolve the Israeli-Palestinian conflict. A two-state solution would involve the establishment of an independent Palestinian state alongside Israel, with mutually agreed-upon borders and security arrangements. This would require Israel to end its occupation of Palestinian territories and dismantle the settlements that have been established in the West Bank. Such a solution would represent a break from the colonial mindset of territorial expansion and control and would allow both Israelis and Palestinians to exercise their right to self-determination.

However, the prospects for a two-state solution have become increasingly uncertain, as the expansion of settlements and the political divisions between Israeli and Palestinian leaders have made it difficult to envision a viable path forward. The ongoing fragmentation of Palestinian territories, with areas under differing degrees of Israeli control, has also complicated the possibility of creating a contiguous and sovereign Palestinian state. The challenge for Israel is to demonstrate a genuine commitment to peace and to address the historical injustices that have been inflicted upon the Palestinian people, including the displacement of refugees and the loss of land and resources.

Another possible path is the pursuit of a one-state solution, in which Israelis and Palestinians would share a single, democratic state with equal rights for all citizens. This solution would require Israel to abandon its identity as an exclusively Jewish state and instead embrace a multicultural, multiethnic identity. While this would represent a significant departure from the original vision of Zionism, it could provide a way to overcome the divisions that have plagued the region for decades and create a society based on equality and shared citizenship. The challenge of achieving such a solution lies in addressing the deep-seated fears and mistrust that exist on both sides, as well as the political and social inequalities that would need to be addressed in order to create a truly inclusive state.

The future of Israel and its colonial heritage will also depend on the role of the international community. The continued support of Western powers, particularly the United States, has enabled Israel to maintain its current policies without facing significant pressure to change. However, there is growing recognition, both within Israel and internationally, that the status quo is unsustainable and that a just resolution to the conflict is necessary for the long-term security and stability of the region. The international community has a role to play in promoting accountability, supporting efforts for reconciliation, and encouraging both sides to engage in meaningful negotiations that can lead to a lasting peace.

Ultimately, the future of Israel will depend on its willingness to confront the legacy of its colonial past and to make the difficult choices necessary to create a just and equitable society for all who live within its borders. Moving beyond the colonial mindset will require a recognition of Palestinian rights, an end to policies of domination and exclusion, and a commitment to building a future based on mutual respect and coexistence. As the last vestige of colonialism in the region, Israel has the opportunity to redefine its place in the 21st century and to become a model for how deeply rooted conflicts can be resolved through dialogue, reconciliation, and a shared vision for the future.

# The Future of Colonial Dynamics in the Middle East

## SHIFTING POWER STRUCTURES

The Middle East is undergoing significant shifts in power structures, and these changes are reshaping the dynamics of colonial legacies in the region. Traditional power dynamics, which were largely shaped by Western colonial influence, are evolving as regional actors seek to assert their own interests and redefine their roles. The decline of Western hegemony in the region, coupled with the emergence of new alliances and rivalries, is creating an environment in which the legacy of colonialism is being reassessed and, in some cases, reimagined.

One of the key factors contributing to the shifting power structures is the rise of regional powers such as Iran, Turkey, and Saudi Arabia, which are increasingly asserting their influence in regional affairs. These countries are actively engaged in shaping the political landscape of the Middle East, often through proxy conflicts, economic investments, and diplomatic initiatives. The rivalry between Iran and Saudi Arabia, in particular, has become a defining feature of regional politics, with both countries vying for influence in countries such as Syria, Yemen, and Iraq. This rivalry is rooted in both sectarian and geopolitical considerations and reflects a broader struggle for dominance in the post-colonial Middle East.

Turkey has also emerged as a significant regional player, seeking to expand its influence through military interventions, soft power, and economic partnerships. Under President Recep Tayyip Erdoğan, Turkey has sought to position itself as a leading power in the Muslim world, challenging traditional Arab leadership and asserting its role in regional conflicts, such as those in Syria and Libya. Turkey's assertive foreign policy is part of a broader effort to reshape the regional order and challenge the legacies of colonialism, particularly in areas that were once part of the Ottoman Empire.

The normalization of relations between Israel and several Arab states through the Abraham Accords is another example of the shifting power structures in the region. The agreements between Israel, the United Arab Emirates, Bahrain, Sudan, and Morocco represent a significant departure from the traditional Arab position of refusing to recognize Israel until a resolution to the Palestinian issue is achieved. These agreements have created new alliances that are reshaping the regional order and have implications for the future of the Palestinian cause. The realignment of alliances reflects a pragmatic approach by some Arab states, who see cooperation with Israel as beneficial for their own security and economic interests, particularly in the face of shared concerns over Iran.

The changing power dynamics in the Middle East have implications for the colonial legacies that continue to affect the region. As regional powers assert their influence, the traditional role of Western countries as the primary arbiters of regional affairs is being challenged. This shift creates opportunities for the region to address historical injustices and to redefine relationships based on mutual interests rather than the legacy of colonial domination. However, it also presents challenges, as the competition for influence among regional powers can exacerbate existing conflicts and create new sources of instability.

### The Role of Regional Powers in Addressing Historical Legacies

The role of regional powers in addressing the historical legacies of colonialism is becoming increasingly important as the Middle East seeks to move beyond its colonial past and build a more stable and just future. Regional actors have the potential to play a leading role in addressing the grievances and inequalities that are rooted in the colonial era, particularly in relation to issues such as borders, resources, and the rights of marginalized populations.

One of the key areas where regional powers can contribute to addressing colonial legacies is in supporting the Palestinian cause. The issue of Palestine is one of the most significant remnants of colonialism in the region, and it remains a central point of contention in Middle Eastern politics. Regional powers, particularly those that have normalized relations with Israel, have a responsibility to use their influence to advocate for a just resolution to the Israeli-Palestinian conflict. This includes supporting efforts to end the occupation, advocating for the rights of Palestinian refugees, and promoting initiatives that foster dialogue and reconciliation. The role of regional powers in mediating between Israel and Palestine could be crucial in creating the conditions for a lasting peace.

In addition to the Palestinian issue, regional powers also have a role to play in addressing the broader economic and social legacies of colonialism. The borders of many Middle Eastern countries were drawn by colonial powers with little regard for the ethnic, religious, and cultural diversity of the region. This has led to internal conflicts and tensions that continue to affect the stability of several countries. Regional actors, such as the Gulf Cooperation Council (GCC) and the Arab League, have the potential to promote greater regional integration and cooperation, which could help to address some of the challenges created by these artificial borders. By fostering economic partnerships, investing in infrastructure, and supporting initiatives that promote cultural exchange, regional powers can contribute to the development of a more interconnected and resilient Middle East.

Reconciliation and addressing historical grievances are also important components of moving beyond the colonial legacy. The legacy of colonialism has left deep scars on the social fabric of many Middle Eastern countries, particularly in relation to ethnic and religious minorities. Regional powers can play a role in promoting inclusive governance and ensuring that the rights of all citizens are protected, regardless of their background. This includes supporting initiatives that promote dialogue between different communities, addressing issues of discrimination and inequality, and ensuring that marginalized groups have a voice in decision-making processes. By promoting inclusivity and addressing historical injustices, regional powers can help to create a more stable and cohesive region.

The future of colonial dynamics in the Middle East will depend on the ability of regional powers to take the lead in addressing the legacies of colonialism and building a new regional order based on cooperation and mutual respect. While the influence of Western powers remains significant, the rise of regional actors and the shifting power structures in the region create opportunities for a new approach to regional governance. By addressing historical grievances, supporting the rights of marginalized populations, and fostering greater regional integration, the Middle East has the potential to move beyond its colonial past and build a future that is defined by justice, stability, and prosperity for all its people.

# Boycotting Israeli Products to Support Palestine and How to Help

## BOYCOTTING ISRAELI Products

The boycott of Israeli products is a strategy employed by those who wish to protest against Israel's occupation of Palestinian territories and its treatment of Palestinians. The boycott aims to put economic pressure on Israel by encouraging consumers, businesses, and governments to refuse to buy products made in Israel or in Israeli settlements in the occupied territories. This form of economic activism is part of the broader Boycott, Divestment, Sanctions (BDS) movement, which seeks to compel Israel to comply with international law and respect Palestinian rights.

One of the main targets of the boycott is products manufactured in Israeli settlements in the West Bank. These settlements are considered illegal under international law, and the expansion of settlements is one of the key obstacles to peace between Israel and Palestine. By refusing to buy products from these areas, consumers can send a message that they do not support the ongoing occupation and the violation of Palestinian rights. Products from settlements are often labeled as "Made in Israel," and consumers are encouraged to educate themselves on which brands and companies operate in these areas in order to avoid supporting them.

In addition to settlement products, the boycott also targets Israeli companies and multinational corporations that are complicit in the occupation. This includes companies that provide services or products used in the construction of settlements, the building of the separation barrier, or the maintenance of checkpoints that restrict Palestinian movement. By boycotting these companies, consumers and organizations aim to increase the economic cost of the occupation and pressure these businesses to change their practices or withdraw from activities that contribute to human rights violations.

The boycott of Israeli products is not only about economic pressure; it is also a tool for raising awareness about the situation in Palestine. By encouraging people to think about the origins of the products they buy and the impact of their purchasing decisions, the boycott helps to educate the public about the realities of the Israeli-Palestinian conflict and the daily hardships faced by Palestinians under occupation. The boycott is a nonviolent form of protest that allows individuals to take a stand in support of Palestinian rights and contribute to the broader struggle for justice.

### How to Help Palestine Beyond Boycotting

In addition to boycotting Israeli products, there are several other ways that individuals and organizations can support the Palestinian cause and help improve the lives of Palestinians living under occupation.

### 1. Support Palestinian Businesses and Products

One way to help Palestinians is by supporting Palestinian businesses and purchasing products made in Palestine. By buying Palestinian goods, consumers can help boost the local economy, create jobs, and provide much-needed income to Palestinian families. Palestinian products, such as olive oil, handicrafts, and cultural items, are often available through fair trade organizations and online marketplaces that prioritize ethical sourcing. Supporting Palestinian businesses helps to strengthen the Palestinian economy and provides an alternative to purchasing goods from Israeli settlements.

### 2. Donate to Organizations Providing Humanitarian Aid

Many organizations are working on the ground in Palestine to provide humanitarian aid to those in need. These organizations provide essential services, such as medical care, food assistance, education, and psychosocial support to Palestinian communities affected by the occupation and conflict. Donating to reputable NGOs, such as

UNRWA (United Nations Relief and Works Agency for Palestine Refugees), Medical Aid for Palestinians, or the Palestinian Red Crescent Society, can make a significant difference in the lives of those living under difficult conditions.

### 3. Advocate for Palestinian Rights

Advocacy is a powerful tool for raising awareness and putting pressure on governments and institutions to take action in support of Palestinian rights. Individuals can contact their elected representatives, participate in protests, sign petitions, and join campaigns calling for an end to the occupation and the recognition of Palestinian rights. Advocacy can also involve challenging biased media coverage and ensuring that the Palestinian perspective is heard in public discourse. By amplifying Palestinian voices and pushing for policy changes, advocates can contribute to the struggle for justice and equality.

### 4. Educate Yourself and Others

Education is an essential aspect of supporting the Palestinian cause. Many people are unaware of the history of the Israeli-Palestinian conflict or the realities of life under occupation. By educating yourself about the situation, you can become a more informed advocate for Palestinian rights. Sharing this knowledge with others, whether through conversations, social media, or community events, helps to raise awareness and build solidarity. Reading books, watching documentaries, and following credible sources of information are all ways to deepen your understanding of the issues at hand.

### 5. Support Cultural and Academic Boycotts

The cultural and academic boycotts of Israel are part of the broader BDS movement and aim to isolate institutions that are complicit in the occupation and the violation of Palestinian rights. Supporting these boycotts means refusing to participate in cultural or academic events sponsored by the Israeli government or institutions that support the occupation. It also involves encouraging artists, academics, and cultural figures to speak out in support of Palestinian rights and to refrain from activities that may normalize the occupation. By supporting the cultural and academic boycotts, individuals can contribute to the effort to pressure Israel to change its policies.

**6. Volunteer with Organizations Supporting Palestinian Rights**

Volunteering your time and skills is another way to support Palestine. Many organizations, both local and international, work to support Palestinian communities, advocate for human rights, and raise awareness about the situation in Palestine. Volunteering with these organizations, whether in person or remotely, can make a meaningful impact. Volunteers can assist with tasks such as organizing events, conducting research, providing educational support, or helping with fundraising efforts.

**7. Push for Divestment from Companies Complicit in the Occupation**

Divestment campaigns target companies that are complicit in the occupation of Palestinian territories and the violation of Palestinian rights. These campaigns call on institutions, such as universities, pension funds, and churches, to divest from companies that profit from the occupation. By supporting divestment campaigns, individuals can help to put financial pressure on these companies and demonstrate that complicity in human rights violations will not be tolerated. Divestment is a powerful tool for holding corporations accountable and challenging the economic structures that sustain the occupation.

The boycott of Israeli products is just one of many ways that individuals can take action in support of Palestinian rights. By combining economic pressure with advocacy, education, and direct support for Palestinian communities, it is possible to make a meaningful contribution to the struggle for justice and equality in Palestine. Each of these actions, whether large or small, helps to build solidarity with the Palestinian people and to challenge the structures of oppression that have denied them their rights for far too long.

# How Countries Can Help Palestine and Pressure Israel

## 1. DIPLOMATIC PRESSURE and Advocacy

Countries can play a significant role in supporting Palestine by using their diplomatic influence to advocate for Palestinian rights on the international stage. Governments can pressure Israel by consistently raising the issue in forums such as the United Nations, the European Union, and other regional organizations. They can push for the adoption of resolutions that condemn Israel's violations of international law and call for an end to the occupation of Palestinian territories.

Countries can also support Palestine by recognizing it as an independent state. Official recognition strengthens the legitimacy of the Palestinian cause and increases pressure on Israel to engage in negotiations aimed at achieving a two-state solution. Governments can open embassies in Palestine and promote bilateral relations to demonstrate their commitment to Palestinian self-determination.

## 2. Sanctions and Trade Restrictions

Economic sanctions are a powerful tool that countries can use to pressure Israel to change its policies. By imposing targeted sanctions on individuals and companies involved in illegal settlement expansion, human rights abuses, and other violations of international law, countries can create financial consequences for actions that undermine the rights of Palestinians. These sanctions can include travel bans, asset freezes, and restrictions on doing business with companies operating in Israeli settlements.

In addition to targeted sanctions, countries can also implement trade restrictions on goods produced in Israeli settlements. By refusing to import products made in the occupied territories, countries can send a clear message that they do not support the illegal settlement enterprise. Governments can also encourage businesses to divest from companies that are complicit in the occupation and call on their own citizens to boycott settlement products.

### 3. Support for International Investigations and Legal Action

Countries can support efforts to hold Israel accountable for alleged war crimes and human rights abuses by endorsing international investigations and legal action. This can include cooperating with investigations conducted by the International Criminal Court (ICC) and supporting resolutions at the United Nations Human Rights Council (UNHRC) that call for independent inquiries into violations committed in the occupied Palestinian territories.

Governments can also provide legal and financial support to Palestinian victims seeking justice in international courts. By helping Palestinians file legal cases against Israeli officials or companies involved in the occupation, countries can contribute to efforts to hold perpetrators accountable and create a deterrent effect against future violations.

### 4. Economic and Humanitarian Assistance to Palestine

Providing economic and humanitarian assistance is an essential way for countries to support the Palestinian people. Many Palestinians face significant economic challenges due to the Israeli blockade of Gaza, restrictions on movement in the West Bank, and the destruction of infrastructure during conflicts. By providing financial aid, countries can help address urgent humanitarian needs, such as food, clean water, healthcare, and housing.

In addition to humanitarian aid, countries can also invest in long-term development projects that promote economic self-sufficiency for Palestinians. This can include funding infrastructure projects, supporting the growth of Palestinian businesses, and providing technical assistance to improve governance and public services. Economic development is crucial for strengthening the resilience of Palestinian communities and reducing their dependency on external assistance.

## 5. Promoting Accountability Through International Forums

Countries can use their influence in international organizations to promote accountability for violations of international law. By voting in favor of resolutions that call for investigations into Israeli actions in the occupied territories, countries can contribute to building international consensus against the occupation. Governments can also support initiatives that call for an end to the blockade of Gaza, the cessation of settlement expansion, and the protection of Palestinian human rights.

Countries can also work to ensure that international aid to Israel is conditioned on compliance with international law. By conditioning military or financial aid on improvements in Israel's treatment of Palestinians, countries can create incentives for positive changes in Israeli policies. This approach has been used in other contexts to encourage governments to respect human rights and adhere to international norms.

## 6. Supporting the Boycott, Divestment, Sanctions (BDS) Movement

The Boycott, Divestment, Sanctions (BDS) movement is a global campaign that seeks to pressure Israel to comply with international law by boycotting Israeli goods, divesting from companies complicit in the occupation, and advocating for sanctions against Israel. Countries can support the BDS movement by adopting policies that discourage businesses from engaging with Israeli settlements or companies involved in human rights abuses. Governments can also implement public procurement policies that exclude companies that are complicit in the occupation.

Supporting the BDS movement at the governmental level can increase pressure on Israel to change its policies and respect Palestinian rights. While some countries have been hesitant to endorse BDS due to political considerations, supporting targeted boycotts of settlement products or companies involved in the occupation is a way to align economic policies with international legal principles.

## 7. Facilitating Peace Talks and Mediation

Countries with diplomatic influence in the region can play a constructive role in facilitating peace talks and mediation between Israel and Palestine. By acting as impartial mediators, countries can help create the conditions for meaningful negotiations and build trust between the parties. Countries can also work with regional actors, such as Egypt and Jordan, to promote a unified approach to the peace process and encourage both sides to make the necessary compromises for a lasting solution.

Facilitating peace talks also involves addressing the power imbalance between Israel and Palestine. To ensure that negotiations are fair and equitable, countries can provide technical and legal support to the Palestinian negotiating team and advocate for the inclusion of international observers to ensure transparency in the process. A credible and balanced mediation process is essential for achieving a just and lasting resolution to the conflict.

## 8. Raising Awareness and Challenging Narratives

Countries can also play a role in supporting Palestine by raising awareness about the situation on the ground and challenging biased narratives. Governments can use their diplomatic platforms to highlight the impact of the occupation on Palestinian lives and advocate for the protection of Palestinian rights. By supporting fact-finding missions, publishing reports on the situation in Palestine, and ensuring that international forums address the issue, countries can help keep the Palestinian struggle for justice and freedom in the global spotlight.

Challenging narratives also involves addressing misinformation and propaganda that may distort the realities of the conflict. Countries can support independent media, human rights organizations, and civil society groups that provide accurate information about the situation in Palestine. Promoting balanced and fact-based discourse on the Israeli-Palestinian conflict is crucial for building international support for Palestinian rights.

Countries have a range of tools at their disposal to support Palestine and pressure Israel to comply with international law. From diplomatic pressure and economic sanctions to providing humanitarian aid and facilitating peace talks, each of these actions can contribute to the broader struggle for justice, equality, and self-determination for the Palestinian people. By taking a principled stand and using their influence to advocate for Palestinian rights, countries can help create the conditions for a just and lasting peace in the region.

# Conclusion

The conclusion brings together the key themes explored throughout the book, summarizing the historical and genetic evidence that reveals the European roots of modern Israel. This evidence paints a picture of Israel as a nation born from a complex interplay of European colonial ambitions, migration patterns, and cultural influences, rather than a straightforward return to an ancestral homeland. The demographic and historical analysis underscores the continuity between European colonial practices and the establishment of Israel, highlighting the displacement of native populations and the cultural dominance of European ideologies.

Israel stands as the last vestige of European colonialism in the Middle East—a unique remnant in a region that has largely undergone decolonization. This position invites a reevaluation of Israel's place in the region, not only in terms of its historical roots but also its current role as a state with ongoing colonial characteristics. The colonial framework through which Israel was established continues to shape its relationships with both neighboring countries and the indigenous Palestinian population, perpetuating dynamics of power, exclusion, and resistance.

Looking ahead, the path to reconciliation and justice requires acknowledging the past and addressing the injustices experienced by marginalized communities. This includes recognizing the displacement of Palestinians, the marginalization of non-European Jewish groups, and the colonial structures that have contributed to ongoing conflicts. Moving forward involves finding ways to bridge divides, promote dialogue, and work toward a just and equitable future for all who live in the region.

The book concludes with a reflection on the broader influence of colonial legacies on the world today. The legacy of European colonialism is not limited to Israel; its impact is felt across the globe, shaping international relations, economic disparities, and cultural narratives. By understanding the colonial past and its lasting influence, there is hope that more equitable and inclusive solutions can be found—not only for Israel and Palestine but for other regions that continue to grapple with the consequences of colonialism.

# Summary of the Historical and Genetic Evidence

## HISTORICAL EVIDENCE of European Involvement in Israel's Formation

The history of Israel's establishment is deeply intertwined with European influence, both in terms of ideology and political support. The Zionist movement, which began in the late 19th century, emerged largely in response to the discrimination and persecution faced by European Jews. This movement sought to establish a Jewish homeland in Palestine, a goal that was significantly influenced by European nationalist ideas. Theodor Herzl, widely regarded as the father of modern Zionism, and other key Zionist leaders were heavily influenced by European political philosophies, which framed the concept of a Jewish state in the context of self-determination and nationhood.

The involvement of European powers in the establishment of Israel was also critical to its success. During World War I, Britain made a series of promises regarding the future of Palestine, most notably through the Balfour Declaration of 1917, which expressed British support for the establishment of a "national home for the Jewish people" in Palestine. After the war, Britain took control of Palestine under the League of Nations mandate system, providing the political environment in which Jewish immigration and settlement in the region could be facilitated. British policies during the mandate period laid the groundwork for the creation of Israel, despite resistance from the indigenous Palestinian population.

After World War II, the horrors of the Holocaust galvanized international support for the establishment of a Jewish state. Many Holocaust survivors and European Jews migrated to Palestine, dramatically altering the demographics of the region. European and American support was crucial during this period, leading to the United

Nations partition plan of 1947, which proposed the division of Palestine into separate Jewish and Arab states. Despite opposition from the Arab population and neighboring states, Israel declared independence in 1948, and its establishment was recognized by major Western powers. The historical context of European support and intervention played a significant role in shaping the modern state of Israel and its ongoing conflict with the Palestinian population.

**Genetic Evidence of European Ancestry in Modern Israelis**

Genetic studies have provided insight into the ancestry of the modern Israeli population, revealing significant European lineage, particularly among Ashkenazi Jews, who make up a large portion of Israel's population. Ashkenazi Jews are descendants of Jewish communities that lived in Europe, particularly in Central and Eastern Europe, for centuries. Genetic research has shown that Ashkenazi Jews share ancestry with both Middle Eastern and European populations, reflecting the history of migration, conversion, and intermarriage that occurred over many generations.

Studies have shown that while Ashkenazi Jews have a genetic link to ancient Jewish populations from the Levant, they also carry a significant proportion of European genetic material, suggesting that their ancestors intermingled with European populations during their centuries-long presence in Europe. This European ancestry is particularly pronounced when compared to other Jewish communities, such as Mizrahi and Sephardic Jews, who have historically lived in the Middle East and North Africa and therefore exhibit a closer genetic affinity to populations from those regions.

The genetic evidence of European ancestry among Ashkenazi Jews provides a counterpoint to the narrative that modern Israelis are returning to their ancestral homeland. While there is undoubtedly a historical connection between the Jewish people and the land of Israel, the genetic diversity of the modern Jewish population, including significant European admixture, complicates the idea of a direct and unbroken link to the ancient inhabitants of the region. This evidence also highlights the diverse origins of the Jewish diaspora and the ways in which centuries of migration and adaptation have shaped the genetic makeup of modern Jewish communities.

The migration of European Jews to Palestine in the late 19th and early 20th centuries, followed by the mass immigration of Holocaust survivors after World War II, significantly influenced the demographics of the region. The establishment of Israel as a predominantly Jewish state was facilitated by this influx of European Jews, who brought with them the cultural, linguistic, and political influences of their countries of origin. This European influence is still evident in many aspects of Israeli society today, from the political institutions to the cultural norms that dominate public life.

## Impact of Historical and Genetic Evidence on the Israeli-Palestinian Conflict

The historical and genetic evidence of European involvement in the formation of Israel and the European ancestry of much of its population has significant implications for understanding the Israeli-Palestinian conflict. The establishment of Israel as a state for the Jewish people, facilitated by European support, came at the expense of the indigenous Palestinian population, who were displaced from their homes and denied their right to self-determination. The influx of European Jews and the subsequent creation of a Jewish state in a region with an existing Arab population have been central to the conflict and the ongoing struggle for Palestinian rights.

The genetic diversity of the Israeli population also challenges the narrative of a homogeneous Jewish people with an exclusive claim to the land. The presence of European ancestry among modern Israelis suggests a complex history of migration and adaptation, rather than a simple return to an ancestral homeland. This complexity is often overlooked in the political discourse surrounding the conflict, which tends to focus on competing historical claims to the land.

Understanding the historical and genetic context of Israel's formation can provide a more nuanced perspective on the conflict and the claims of both Israelis and Palestinians. It highlights the role of European colonialism in shaping the modern Middle East and the ways in which historical injustices continue to affect the lives of millions of people today. Addressing these historical legacies is essential for achieving a just and lasting resolution to the conflict, one that acknowledges the rights and aspirations of both Israelis and Palestinians.

# The Last Vestige of European Colonialism: Reevaluating Israel's Place in the Region

**HISTORICAL CONTEXT of European Colonialism and Israel's Establishment**

The establishment of Israel in 1948 is often viewed through the lens of European colonialism, as it involved the intervention of Western powers, the displacement of the indigenous Palestinian population, and the subsequent creation of a state that aligned itself more closely with Western values and interests than with the Middle Eastern context. The historical roots of Israel's establishment can be traced back to the Zionist movement of the late 19th century, which emerged in response to the persecution of Jews in Europe. Influenced by European nationalist ideologies, Zionist leaders sought to establish a Jewish homeland in Palestine, a region with an existing Arab population that had lived there for generations.

The role of European powers in facilitating the creation of Israel cannot be overstated. The Balfour Declaration of 1917, in which the British government expressed support for a "national home for the Jewish people" in Palestine, laid the groundwork for the future state of Israel. Following World War I, Britain took control of Palestine under the mandate system, providing political support and enabling Jewish immigration to the region. This period of British rule saw significant tension between the Jewish and Arab populations, with the British ultimately struggling to manage the conflicting nationalist aspirations.

After World War II, the horrors of the Holocaust led to increased international support for the establishment of a Jewish state, and many European Jews migrated to Palestine. The United Nations partition plan of 1947, which proposed dividing Palestine into separate Jewish and Arab states, was supported by major Western powers but rejected by the Arab population and neighboring countries. The declaration of Israeli independence in 1948 and the ensuing Arab-Israeli War led to the displacement of hundreds of thousands of Palestinians, known as the Nakba ("catastrophe"), and the beginning of an ongoing conflict that continues to shape the region today.

**Israel's Place in the Middle East: A European Legacy**

Israel's establishment and subsequent development have often been characterized as the last vestige of European colonialism in the Middle East. Unlike other post-colonial nations in the region, Israel was created with significant backing from Western powers, both politically and militarily. This Western support has continued throughout Israel's history, with the United States and European countries providing economic aid, military assistance, and diplomatic backing. The perception of Israel as a Western outpost in the Middle East has contributed to its complicated relationship with its Arab neighbors, many of whom view Israel as an extension of Western imperialism.

The European influence on Israel is evident in its political, cultural, and economic systems. Israel adopted Western-style democratic institutions, developed a market-based economy, and aligned itself with Western countries during the Cold War and beyond. This alignment has often placed Israel at odds with its Middle Eastern neighbors, many of whom have experienced their own struggles with Western colonialism and imperialism. The cultural influence of Europe is also visible in Israeli society, with European languages, customs, and values playing a significant role in shaping the country's identity, particularly among the Ashkenazi Jewish population, which has historically held significant political and economic power.

The ongoing occupation of Palestinian territories, the expansion of Israeli settlements, and the treatment of Palestinians have further reinforced the perception of Israel as a colonial power. The settlements in the West Bank are often viewed as a continuation of the colonial practice of expropriating land and resources for the benefit of the colonizer. The separation barrier, checkpoints, and restrictions on Palestinian movement are seen as measures to maintain control over an indigenous population, echoing the practices of European colonial authorities in their colonies.

### Reevaluating Israel's Role in the Region

As the Middle East undergoes significant geopolitical changes, Israel's place in the region is being reevaluated. The normalization of relations between Israel and several Arab states through the Abraham Accords represents a shift in regional dynamics, as countries such as the United Arab Emirates, Bahrain, Sudan, and Morocco have chosen to establish diplomatic ties with Israel despite the ongoing Israeli-Palestinian conflict. These agreements reflect a pragmatic approach by some Arab states, prioritizing economic and security interests over solidarity with the Palestinian cause. This realignment suggests that Israel may be moving away from its image as an isolated entity in the Middle East and becoming more integrated into the regional framework.

However, this process of normalization does not negate the legacy of colonialism that continues to shape Israel's relationship with the Palestinians. The occupation of the West Bank, the blockade of Gaza, and the ongoing expansion of settlements remain significant obstacles to peace and contribute to the perception of Israel as a colonial power. Addressing these issues is essential for Israel to redefine its role in the region and move beyond its colonial legacy. This would require a genuine commitment to ending the occupation, recognizing Palestinian rights, and working toward a just and equitable resolution to the conflict.

The reevaluation of Israel's place in the region also involves acknowledging the diversity of its own population. While Israel has historically been dominated by European-descended Ashkenazi Jews, the country is home to a diverse population that includes Mizrahi Jews from the Middle East and North Africa, Ethiopian Jews, and Arab citizens of Israel. Recognizing and valuing this diversity is crucial for Israel to build a more inclusive society that reflects its location in the Middle East rather than its European origins. By embracing its multicultural identity, Israel can work to bridge the gap between itself and its neighbors and foster a sense of belonging within the region.

For Israel to truly move beyond its colonial legacy, it must also engage in reconciliation with the Palestinian people. This involves acknowledging the historical injustices that have been inflicted upon the Palestinian population, including the displacement of refugees, the loss of land, and the denial of basic rights. Reconciliation requires not only political agreements but also a process of truth-telling, recognition, and reparative justice. By addressing the grievances of the past, Israel and Palestine can work toward building a future based on mutual respect and coexistence.

The reevaluation of Israel's place in the Middle East is an ongoing process that requires a willingness to confront difficult truths about the past and make meaningful changes for the future. As the last vestige of European colonialism in the region, Israel has the opportunity to redefine its role and become a partner for peace and stability. This will require addressing the root causes of the Israeli-Palestinian conflict, ending the occupation, and working toward a just resolution that respects the rights and aspirations of both Israelis and Palestinians.

Only then can Israel move beyond its colonial heritage and take its place as an integral part of the Middle East.

# Moving Forward: Acknowledging the Past and Seeking Justice

## ACKNOWLEDGING HISTORICAL Injustices

To move forward in the pursuit of justice for Palestinians, it is crucial to acknowledge the historical injustices that have taken place since the establishment of Israel. The 1948 Nakba, which led to the displacement of over 700,000 Palestinians, resulted in the destruction of hundreds of Palestinian villages and the forced exile of countless families from their homes. These actions, carried out to create the state of Israel, are at the core of the Palestinian struggle for justice and recognition.

The establishment of Israel was facilitated by Western colonial powers, with little regard for the rights of the indigenous Palestinian population. The ongoing Israeli occupation of the West Bank, the annexation of East Jerusalem, and the blockade of Gaza are manifestations of Israel's colonial project, which continues to deny Palestinians their fundamental rights. Recognizing these injustices is a crucial step in dismantling the structures of oppression that have been imposed on Palestinians for over seven decades.

Israel's policies of land expropriation, settlement expansion, and ethnic cleansing have led to the systemic marginalization and dispossession of Palestinians. Acknowledging these crimes is essential for any path toward justice. Israel was established on Palestinian land, and the Zionist project has consistently sought to expand at the expense of the indigenous population. This colonial endeavor must be addressed by recognizing the illegitimacy of Israel's claims to Palestinian land.

### The Pursuit of Justice for Palestinians

Justice for Palestinians begins with recognizing that Israel, as a colonial entity, has no legitimate right to Palestinian land. The land of historic Palestine belongs to the Palestinian people, who have lived there for generations. The continued occupation and settlement of Palestinian territories by Israel are in violation of international law and must come to an end. Justice requires the complete decolonization of Palestine and the restoration of Palestinian sovereignty over their land.

The right of return for Palestinian refugees is central to achieving justice. The forced displacement of Palestinians during the Nakba and subsequent conflicts has created one of the largest and longest-standing refugee crises in the world. These refugees have the right to return to their homes, as recognized by international law. Justice demands that Israel acknowledge the right of return and facilitate the return of Palestinian refugees to their ancestral lands.

Ending the blockade of Gaza and the military occupation of the West Bank is also critical to achieving justice for Palestinians. The blockade of Gaza has created a humanitarian crisis, depriving Palestinians of basic necessities, such as clean water, electricity, and medical supplies. The occupation of the West Bank has led to the confiscation of Palestinian land, the destruction of homes, and the imposition of severe restrictions on movement. Justice requires the lifting of the blockade, the withdrawal of Israeli forces, and the dismantling of settlements.

Justice for Palestinians also involves holding Israel accountable for its actions. This means prosecuting those responsible for war crimes and human rights abuses, whether they are political leaders, military officials, or settlers. The international community must support investigations by the International Criminal Court (ICC) and other international bodies to ensure that those responsible for the ongoing oppression of Palestinians are held accountable.

**Building a Future Based on Justice and Restoring Palestinian Rights**

Moving forward requires not only addressing past injustices but also building a future that restores the rights of the Palestinian people. This includes dismantling the apartheid system that Israel has established, which privileges Jewish Israelis at the expense of Palestinians. Equality must be the foundation of any future political system in Palestine, with all people—regardless of their religion or ethnicity—enjoying the same rights and freedoms.

Restoring Palestinian sovereignty involves ending Israel's control over all aspects of Palestinian life, including borders, natural resources, and governance. Palestinians must have the right to determine their own future, free from Israeli interference. This means dismantling the structures of occupation, including checkpoints, the separation barrier, and military zones that restrict Palestinian movement and development.

Grassroots initiatives and Palestinian-led movements play an essential role in the fight for justice. The Palestinian people have consistently resisted Israeli colonization through various forms of resistance, including protests, strikes, and international advocacy. Supporting Palestinian resistance efforts and amplifying Palestinian voices are crucial to the struggle for liberation. Solidarity with Palestinian-led movements, such as the Boycott, Divestment, Sanctions (BDS) movement, is an important way for individuals and organizations around the world to support the fight for justice.

**International Support for Justice and Accountability**

The international community must take a principled stand in support of Palestinian rights and against Israeli colonialism. This includes imposing sanctions on Israel, ending military aid, and boycotting Israeli products. The continued support of Israel by Western countries, particularly the United States, has enabled Israel to maintain its colonial project without facing consequences. The international community must hold Israel accountable for its actions and take concrete steps to end its impunity.

Countries must also support Palestinian efforts for self-determination by recognizing Palestine as a sovereign state and advocating for the end of the occupation. Recognition of Palestine sends a powerful message that the Palestinian people have a legitimate right to their land and that the international community stands in solidarity with their struggle for justice. Governments and international organizations must also support Palestinian refugees by advocating for their right of return and providing the necessary resources to facilitate their return.

Justice for Palestinians requires a complete rejection of Israel's colonial claims and the restoration of Palestinian sovereignty over their land. Moving forward involves dismantling the structures of oppression, holding Israel accountable for its crimes, and supporting Palestinian-led efforts for liberation. The path to justice is not through compromise with a colonial power but through the recognition of Palestinian rights, the decolonization of Palestine, and the establishment of a future based on equality and justice for all.

# Final Thoughts on the Global Influence of Colonial Legacies

THE INFLUENCE OF COLONIAL legacies continues to shape global politics, economies, and social structures in the 21st century. The colonial era may have officially ended decades ago, but the impact of European colonialism is still evident in many regions of the world. Colonialism not only redrew borders and disrupted societies but also imposed power dynamics that persist to this day, affecting countries' development, conflicts, and the distribution of resources.

One of the most glaring examples of a lingering colonial legacy is the Israeli-Palestinian conflict. Israel's establishment as a state was facilitated by European powers, with little regard for the existing indigenous Palestinian population. The creation of Israel, and the subsequent displacement of hundreds of thousands of Palestinians, represents a continuation of colonial practices in the modern era. The support of Western nations for Israel, both politically and economically, reflects a colonial mindset in which powerful countries impose their will on weaker populations without regard for their rights and sovereignty.

The legacy of colonialism is also evident in the way global power structures are still largely dominated by Western countries. Many of the institutions that govern international relations, such as the United Nations, the International Monetary Fund, and the World Bank, were established by colonial powers and continue to reflect the interests of those nations. The veto power held by a few countries in the United Nations Security Council, for example, allows former colonial powers to influence global decision-making and maintain their dominance. This concentration of power has often been used to protect allies, such as Israel, from accountability for their actions.

Economic inequality between the Global North and the Global South is another aspect of the colonial legacy. Colonial powers extracted resources from their colonies and built wealth on the backs of colonized peoples, leaving these regions impoverished and underdeveloped. Today, many former colonies continue to struggle with poverty, lack of infrastructure, and economic dependency on their former colonizers. The global economic system, characterized by unfair trade practices and exploitative labor conditions, perpetuates the inequalities that were established during the colonial era.

The concept of racial hierarchy, which was central to colonial ideology, still influences societies around the world. Colonizers justified their exploitation of other peoples by claiming racial superiority, and this belief in racial hierarchy has persisted long after the end of colonial rule. Systemic racism, discrimination, and the marginalization of indigenous populations are direct consequences of colonial attitudes that placed certain groups above others. In Israel, the treatment of Palestinians and the discriminatory policies that favor Jewish settlers over the indigenous population reflect these lingering colonial attitudes.

Addressing the global influence of colonial legacies requires a commitment to decolonization in all its forms—political, economic, and cultural. Politically, this means supporting the rights of oppressed peoples to self-determination, whether in Palestine or in other regions where colonial-era borders and power structures continue to fuel conflict. Economically, it requires challenging the global systems that maintain inequality and working toward a fairer distribution of resources. Wealthy nations must acknowledge their historical role in creating global poverty and take meaningful steps to address these injustices through reparations, debt relief, and support for sustainable development.

Culturally, decolonization means challenging the narratives that continue to justify colonial practices and recognizing the value of indigenous knowledge and perspectives. This involves reassessing history from the viewpoint of the colonized, rather than the colonizer, and giving a voice to those who have been silenced for too long. The glorification of colonial figures and the erasure of the atrocities they committed must be replaced with an honest reckoning of the past and an acknowledgment of the resilience and contributions of colonized peoples.

The influence of colonial legacies is not confined to the past; it is a present reality that continues to affect millions of people around the world. Whether in the ongoing struggle for Palestinian rights, the economic exploitation of the Global South, or the systemic racism that persists in many societies, the impact of colonialism remains pervasive. Moving forward requires a commitment to justice, equality, and the dismantling of the power structures that have kept the world divided for so long. Only by confronting the colonial past and actively working toward a decolonized future can true global justice and peace be achieved.

# Appendix

K ey Historical Documents
      The Balfour Declaration

The Balfour Declaration was a letter dated November 2, 1917, from British Foreign Secretary Arthur Balfour to Lord Rothschild, a leader of the British Jewish community, expressing the British government's support for the establishment of a "national home for the Jewish people" in Palestine. This document is considered one of the key milestones in the history of the Israeli-Palestinian conflict, as it provided international legitimacy to the Zionist movement's goals. The declaration, however, also promised to protect the rights of the non-Jewish communities in Palestine, though this provision was often overlooked in subsequent policies. The Balfour Declaration played a central role in the eventual establishment of Israel and the displacement of Palestinians.

**UN Resolutions on Palestine and Israel**

Throughout the Israeli-Palestinian conflict, the United Nations has passed numerous resolutions addressing the situation. Some of the key resolutions include:

- **UN General Assembly Resolution 181 (1947):** This resolution called for the partition of Palestine into separate Jewish and Arab states, with Jerusalem under international administration. The plan was accepted by the Jewish community but rejected by the Arab states, leading to the outbreak of war in 1948.

- **UN Security Council Resolution 242 (1967):** Passed in the aftermath of the Six-Day War, this resolution called for the withdrawal of Israeli armed forces from territories occupied during the conflict and emphasized the need for "a just and lasting peace" in the region. It has been a cornerstone in peace negotiations ever since.

- **UN General Assembly Resolution 194 (1948):** This resolution affirmed the right of Palestinian refugees to return to their homes and called for compensation for those who chose not to return. The right of return remains a core demand of the Palestinian people.

**Genetic Study Summaries**
**Key Findings on the Ancestry of Modern Israelis**
Multiple genetic studies have examined the ancestry of modern Israelis, particularly Ashkenazi Jews, who form a significant portion of the Israeli population. These studies have revealed that while Ashkenazi Jews have ancestry linked to ancient Jewish populations from the Levant, a significant portion of their genetic makeup reflects European influence due to centuries of migration and intermarriage.

For example, a 2013 study published in *Nature Communications* found that about half of the Ashkenazi Jewish genome comes from European populations, particularly Southern Europe, with the other half tracing back to Middle Eastern populations. This mixture reflects the complex history of the Jewish diaspora, which involved movement through Europe and the Middle East over centuries.

Other studies, such as those examining the genetic makeup of Mizrahi and Sephardic Jews, show a closer connection to populations in the Middle East and North Africa, highlighting the diversity of Jewish communities and their varied historical paths. These findings challenge simplistic narratives about the "return" to an ancestral homeland, underscoring the complex demographic history of modern Israelis.

**Glossary of Terms Related to Colonialism, Zionism, and International Relations**

**Colonialism:** A system of domination in which a foreign power establishes control over a territory and its people, often exploiting resources and suppressing the rights of the indigenous population. Colonialism typically involves settlement, economic exploitation, and cultural domination.

**Zionism:** A nationalist movement that emerged in the late 19th century advocating for the establishment of a Jewish homeland in Palestine. Zionism was driven by the desire to create a safe haven for Jews in response to persecution and anti-Semitism in Europe. While originally a political movement, Zionism has taken on different forms over time, including cultural and religious Zionism.

**Nakba:** Arabic for "catastrophe," Nakba refers to the mass displacement of Palestinians during the 1948 Arab-Israeli War, when hundreds of thousands of Palestinians were expelled from their homes or fled, many of whom became permanent refugees.

**Apartheid:** A system of institutionalized racial segregation and discrimination, originally associated with South Africa. In the context of Israel and Palestine, apartheid refers to policies and practices that favor Jewish settlers and citizens over Palestinians, restricting Palestinian rights and movement in the occupied territories.

**BDS (Boycott, Divestment, Sanctions):** A global movement that seeks to pressure Israel to comply with international law by advocating for boycotts of Israeli products, divestment from companies that support Israeli policies, and sanctions against the Israeli government. The movement is modeled after the anti-apartheid struggle in South Africa.

**Right of Return:** Refers to the principle that Palestinian refugees who were displaced during the 1948 Nakba and subsequent conflicts have the right to return to their original homes. The right of return is enshrined in UN General Assembly Resolution 194 and remains a core issue in the Israeli-Palestinian conflict.

**Self-Determination:** The right of a people to determine their own political status and pursue their own economic, social, and cultural development. For Palestinians, self-determination involves the establishment of an independent state and control over their own land and resources.

**International Criminal Court (ICC):** A permanent international court established to prosecute individuals for genocide, war crimes, crimes against humanity, and crimes of aggression. The ICC has opened investigations into alleged war crimes committed by both Israeli and Palestinian actors in the occupied territories.

# Bibliography

**A**cademic Sources

1. Pappe, Ilan. *The Ethnic Cleansing of Palestine*. Oneworld Publications, 2006.

○ This book provides an in-depth historical analysis of the events leading to the displacement of Palestinians during the 1948 Nakba, highlighting the role of Zionist forces in the ethnic cleansing of Palestinian villages.

2. Said, Edward W. *The Question of Palestine*. Vintage, 1992.

○ Edward Said offers a detailed critique of the Israeli-Palestinian conflict, examining the roots of Zionism, the colonial legacy, and the plight of the Palestinian people.

3. Khalidi, Rashid. *The Iron Cage: The Story of the Palestinian Struggle for Statehood*. Beacon Press, 2007.

○ Khalidi provides a historical overview of the Palestinian struggle for statehood, highlighting the impact of British colonial policies and subsequent Israeli actions.

4. Morris, Benny. *1948: A History of the First Arab-Israeli War*. Yale University Press, 2008.

o This book details the events of the 1948 war, offering insights into the dynamics of the conflict and the displacement of Palestinian communities.

## Historical Records

1. *The Balfour Declaration*, November 2, 1917.

o The letter from British Foreign Secretary Arthur Balfour to Lord Rothschild expressing support for the establishment of a "national home for the Jewish people" in Palestine.

2. United Nations General Assembly Resolution 181 (1947).

o The UN resolution that proposed the partition of Palestine into separate Jewish and Arab states, laying the groundwork for the establishment of Israel.

3. United Nations Security Council Resolution 242 (1967).

o The resolution adopted after the Six-Day War, calling for Israeli withdrawal from occupied territories and emphasizing the need for peace and security in the region.

4. United Nations General Assembly Resolution 194 (1948).

o The resolution affirming the right of Palestinian refugees to return to their homes and calling for compensation for those who choose not to return.

## Genetic Studies

1. Ostrer, Harry. "Abraham's Children in the Genome Era: Major Jewish Diaspora Populations Comprise Distinct Genetic Clusters with Shared Middle Eastern Ancestry." *American Journal of Human Genetics*, vol. 86, no. 6, 2010, pp. 850-859.

○ This study examines the genetic relationships between major Jewish populations, including Ashkenazi Jews, revealing shared Middle Eastern ancestry along with significant European admixture.

2. Behar, Doron M., et al. "The Genome-Wide Structure of the Jewish People." *Nature*, vol. 466, 2010, pp. 238-242.

○ The study provides evidence of the diverse genetic backgrounds of Jewish populations, including Middle Eastern, European, and North African influences.

3. Elhaik, Eran. "The Missing Link of Jewish European Ancestry: Contrasting the Rhineland and the Khazarian Hypotheses." *Genome Biology and Evolution*, vol. 5, no. 1, 2013, pp. 61-74.

○ This study challenges traditional views on the origins of Ashkenazi Jews, suggesting significant European influence and a complex ancestry.

**Political Analyses**

1. Chomsky, Noam, and Ilan Pappe. *Gaza in Crisis: Reflections on Israel's War Against the Palestinians.* Haymarket Books, 2010.

○ Chomsky and Pappe provide an analysis of Israel's policies toward Gaza, examining the broader geopolitical context and the role of Western powers in supporting Israel.

2. Shlaim, Avi. *The Iron Wall: Israel and the Arab World.* W.W. Norton & Company, 2001.

○ Shlaim analyzes Israel's foreign policy and its relationships with neighboring Arab countries, highlighting the influence of colonial legacies on the region's political dynamics.

3. Finkelstein, Norman G. *The Holocaust Industry: Reflections on the Exploitation of Jewish Suffering.* Verso, 2000.

○ Finkelstein critiques the political use of the Holocaust to justify Israeli policies and explores the broader implications for Israeli-Palestinian relations.

4. Masalha, Nur. *Expulsion of the Palestinians: The Concept of "Transfer" in Zionist Political Thought, 1882-1948.* Institute for Palestine Studies, 1992.

○ This book traces the development of the concept of population transfer in Zionist thought, providing context for the mass displacement of Palestinians during the establishment of Israel.

5. Benvenisti, Meron. *Sacred Landscape: The Buried History of the Holy Land Since 1948.* University of California Press, 2000.

○ Benvenisti offers a detailed account of the transformation of the landscape of Palestine, documenting the destruction of Palestinian villages and the erasure of Palestinian cultural heritage.